BARTHOLOMEW START

This book is dedicated to anyone who has been 'caught short'. I trust you can feel a certain empathy for my plight.

Needing an evacuation in Milton Keynes can be just as harrowing as wanting one in Marrakesh. Though, it is far more likely in the latter!

Continue to poo as long as you live, it is something you will never tire of, and it will give you hours of pleasure.

Reliving your 'stool' tales down the pub can make for a memorable night.

Ironically at this point, you will probably be sitting on a stool.

Happy crapping!

Don't forget to wipe your bottom!

Too much blood on the toilet paper means you are wiping too hard!

Concisely wipe – it plays dividends!

Drink plenty of fluids – it helps pass smoothly!

All the best

From BARTHOLOMEW START

THE AUTHOR

Bartholomew Start - Did not have the best 'start' in life. He was born at the fairground in Liverpool, to a family of traveling circus folk, who were performing there in 1963.

He was a nervous child, but he put that down to the fact his mother was fired out of a cannon whilst pregnant.

Born prematurely and virtually blind, he was forced to wear beer bottle spectacles as a child. Consequently, he didn't mix well.

He was in and out of schools - due to his parent's wanderlust. He started to read about nuclear fusion in his spare time. He told his fellow schoolmates he was off to Cambridge. In 1981, he finally got there - his parent's circus act took them to the outskirts of Huntingdon.

His fascination with pooing began very early. Believe it or not, he started pooing the day he was born. By the age of two, he was wiping his bottom, though not very concisely, and by the age of four was toilet trained and never had another accident until he started traveling at the age of eighteen.

Bartholomew currently lives in Liverpool with his family, and despite being elderly, continues to poo most days, much to the delight of his daughter, who seems to be a chip off the old block, as she likes nothing better than having a good 'dump', then telling everyone about it.

CAUGHT SHORT ABROAD is his first book.

THE AUTHOR'S CUT

If you ever watch a classic film, several years after its release the Director will bring out the DIRECTORS CUT version.

This is the film he wanted to make in the first place, before the producers and the censors told him to take out this or that, and put in scenes in the film he left on the cutting room floor.

It is the film he wanted the cinemagoers to see from the start. It is a better film for it.

In my Author cut, I have done the opposite of a Director' cut.

I did manage to pass O level English Language and the same in English Literature, however, that does not make me a worthy author.

Coming from Liverpool I tend to write down things in the same way I talk, and I am a lot better at talking than writing. Sadly, the purists of the English word frown upon such grammatical chaos.

I must say that since I first wrote this book, online spell-checking has improved and I have recently installed a software tool called GRAMMARLY.

Embarrassingly, the software tool picked up well over a thousand grammatical errors in my original. That equates to nearly 10 errors a page. Shakespeare would turn in his grave. James Joyce would have a fit. E.L James might say "spot on" but have you read her books?

So I realized that if I put all the grammatical errors on one page it would look like a morse code manual.

I will add that GRAMMARLY isn't perfect as it corrects the English to American spelling - everyone knows it is humour, not humor, and night not nite, colour not color. But these are the foibles of the English language.

I might add that whilst the book may read better, I do not think it has improved it, indeed possibly the reverse.

In the Author's cut version, I have also added several new chapters to the original never printed before, so I hope they keep you entertained.

Enjoy and remember, we all have to go.

ADVICE OFTEN OVERLOOKED

WARNING - REMOVE TROUSERS BEFORE USE

DON'T FORGET TO WIPE YOUR BOTTOM

REMEMBER A CONCISE WIPER IS A CONTENTED WIPER

ALWAYS LOOK BEHIND YOU PRIOR TO FLUSHING

TOO MUCH BLOOD ON TOILET PAPER MEANS   YOU ARE WIPING TOO HARD

For Hannah & Siobhan

Dedicated to Margaret and Ray

This book was written as a collection of totally unrelated short stories, based on the author's real-life issues in the toilet department, when traveling on a very small budget, in some remote corners of the world, where hygiene and cleanliness are not a priority.

It is not the author's intention to write a travel documentary or a novel.

These stories are not meant to offend the reader in any way.

The style of writing is raw and deliberate, it is written in an anecdotal style, and the grammar may not be to the liking of English teachers, and grammatically, the book is as raw as the subject matter.

Please read this book in the manner it was intended, with a smile on your face.

Everyone goes to the toilet: it is a fact of life. Everyone, whoever you are, have at some point been CAUGHT SHORT, and whilst it may not have been amusing at the time, I am sure you will have seen the funny side since.

If you do not like toilet humour, read no further.

However, if you do, forget your troubles for a few hours and have a good laugh or grimace.

Bartholomew Start

CHAPTERS

CHAPTER ONE – PLEASED TO MEET POO

CHAPTER POO – THE LORD WORKS IN MYSTERIOUS WAYS

CHAPTER THREE – THE LANGUAGE OF LVOV

CHAPTER FOUR – DROP YOUR GUTS

CHAPTER FIVE – LAND OF THE MIDNIGHT FLATULENCE

CHAPTER SIX – WHERE'S MY TROUSERS?

CHAPTER SEVEN – AND HOW WOULD YOU LIKE THAT WRAPPED SIR?

CHAPTER EIGHT – A GOOD JOBBIE

CHAPTER NINE - CHINESE POO?

CHAPTER TEN - THE GOAN PIGS

CHAPTER ELEVEN - BUSES ALWAYS COME IN NUMBER TWOS

CHAPTER TWELVE - KING JUAN CARLOS MEETS DRACULA

CHAPTER THIRTEEN – FLYING BY THE SEAT OF YOUR PANTS

CHAPTER FOURTEEN – TURN LEFT AT BIFFINS BRIDGE

CHAPTER FIFTEEN – BORED SHITLESS

CHAPTER SIXTEEN – SET IT FREE

CHAPTER SEVENTEEN – RED ALERT!

CHAPTER EIGHTEEN – THE GREAT ESCAPE

CHAPTER NINETEEN – RIDE INTO HELL!

CHAPTER TWENTY - TERRY WAITES ALLOTMENT

CHAPTER TWENTY-ONE - BRAZILIANS ARE SHITE

CHAPTER TWENTY-TWO - ABSOLUTE BLISS!

CHAPTER TWENTY-THREE – RETURN TO SENDER

CHAPTER TWENTY-FOUR – SHITTING THROUGH THE EYE OF A NEEDLE

CHAPTER TWENTY- FIVE – WHAT A DUMP!

CHAPTER TWENTY-SIX – PEEL A GRAPE

CHAPTER TWENTY – SEVEN - JOHN HOLMES EAT YOUR HEART OUT

CHAPTER TWENTY- EIGHT - YOU CAN TELL ME I'M A DOCTOR

CHAPTER TWENTY-NINE - HOVIS (GREAT BREAD) TERROBLE BOG PAPER

CHAPTER THIRTY – NOISY NEIGHBOURS

CHAPTER THIRTY-ONE - SECRET AGENT NUMBER 2 BOND!

BASILDON BOND!

CHAPTER THIRTY-TWO – GRANDAD'S THROWEL

CHAPTER THIRTY – THREE – FLUFF'S BOTTOM

CHAPTER THIRTY- FOUR – TURD IN A PHONE BOX

CHAPTER THIRTY-FIVE – A HAZEL NUT IN EVERY BITE

CHAPTER THIRTY – SIX –SATURDAY NIGHT FEVER MY ARSE

CHAPTER THIRTY – SEVEN – STEER CLEAR OF BROWN SNOW

CHAPTER THIRTY- EIGHT – TERRIBLE PHOTOGRAPHS

CHAPTER THIRTY- NINE – SOOTH MY ITCHY ARSE

CHAPTER FORTY – THE SWISS CHOCOLATIER!

CHAPTER FORTY-ONE- TARKI BELAIDAKIS' PILES

CHAPTER FORTY – TWO – SHIT STINKS!

CHAPTER FORTY – THREE – I'VE BEEN DRIVING IN MY CAR

CHAPTER FORTY – FOUR MONKEY BUSINESS

CHAPTER FORTY- FIVE - HATS OFF TO PAULA RADCLIFFE

To........

Message..............

From ....

CRAPOMETER

Ghost Poo - the perfect poo, no effort, no waste, no flush, and no wiping

The Brick - This is the stuff of nightmares, needs an epidural to pass it- This would spook Freddy Kruger!

Killer Poo - the poo with corners on it. Who said you can't fit a square peg in a round hole?

Striped Poo – usually a two-day-old poo that starts out one colour and ends up tapering to a few shades lighter or darker

Sultana Poo – a most disappointing effort, spend half an hour pushing and the result is a sheep size dropping in the bottom of the pan

The Elvis killer – pokes out the top of the water line and has trouble being flushed. This usually happens when visiting relatives.

Hot Tar Poo – sticks like shit to a blanket, after 50 wipes, there is always a bit more.

Second Thought Poo – Just when you think you've finished, trousers go up, and moments later down they go, for a second sitting

The Titanic - breaks up when hitting the water, and resides in the U bend waiting to be salvaged

The Heartbreak poo – a real tear jerker after a spicy curry

Fisherman Poo – No matter how many times you flush, it keeps bobbing to the surface. Usually needs plenty of toilet paper to weigh it down.The fisherman's poo often means too much fat in your diet.

Gozilla Poo – This one is the real deal. Not to be taken lightly, if internal damage has been avoided, a phone call to home serve certainly has not!

"*Pleased to meet Poo*"

Meeting the 'in-laws' for the very first time can be a harrowing experience, especially when you don't speak the 'lingo'.

My girlfriend was Polish, in the days before the Polish Armada arrived on our shores. At the time, people joked I had got her in a magazine for lonely hearts. How the hell did they find out?

In 1990, an Englishman arriving in a small town in Central Poland was a bit of a novelty. Indeed, only a year earlier an exchange student from Tanzania, had caused mayhem when he appeared in the town square, as hundreds of locals, literally hung out of their windows, to 'gawp' at the dark stranger from warmer climes. My arrival behind the Iron Curtain' was a little less newsworthy.

The town of Blonie is just outside Warsaw and has a rather dubious reputation, in a country known for its excessive drinking for being the alcohol capital of Poland

Napoleon had stayed the night in Blonie *en route* to conquering Prussia, and had remarked,

"This is a dull little town in the middle of nowhere".

I expect his famous phrase: "Not tonight Josephine" referred to his not wanting to stay more than a single night in Blonie.

There were drunkards everywhere, queuing for food, serving in shops, driving buses, and serving communion at mass. Everyone was inebriated. It was quite difficult to find anyone who wasn't under the influence of drink. Even dogs in the street were half-cut. Hordes of bison-breathed locals swigging neat alcohol out of brown paper bags, hanging around street corners, shouting obscenities at passing old ladies, and generally knocking seven bells out of each other - and that was the local police force. It made me smile, as I thought perhaps all the propaganda about life behind the Iron Curtain might just be true.

Hindsight is all well and good, and yes with hindsight, I should have gone to the toilet in Denmark or at least on the plane. It had been a long time since the flight left Copenhagen and I knew I needed the toilet just after we left Warsaw International airport, but always think I'll wait.

Four hours later as I walked up the path of the family home in the Polish countryside I was virtually 'touching cloth'. There was a turtles head brewing and there was nothing I could do to coax it back up.

I raced into the house and formally, if a little speedily was introduced to the waiting crowd. After a few minutes of nodding and hand shaking, I found myself alone in a bathroom, which had seen better days. Now I must warn you that the plumbing system in Poland at the time, left a lot to be desired, and the toilet flush was not the most powerful.

After I had finished my ablutions, I returned to the kitchen, where my girlfriend made me a cup of tea, told me to relax, and went out of the room.

A few minutes passed when I heard a commotion near the bathroom. I got up and went to see what all the shouting was about, after all, Polish people having a serious discussion - when you don't understand a word - always seems more dramatic.

To my horror there were four people in the bathroom, all looking down the toilet, having what appeared to be quite a heated debate, her auntie had a broom handle and was forcing it down the toilet and babbling in forked tongues.

The smell was atrocious and made the situation far worse by the fact that my new in-law, in the ceremonial act of breaking up my 'Elvis killer' into fertilizer bite-size chunks, released a fetid fog into the atmosphere that would have stopped a clock.

Her mother, who minutes earlier didn't know me from Adam, sounded quite cross, as she held her head in her hands, as though she had just seen her husband shot by a sniper, so I asked my girlfriend what everyone was saying.

She told me, that her mum was rather perturbed by an enormous turd that had blocked the toilet, and 'someone' had used too much toilet paper. At this point, they all turned and looked at me. I put my head down in shame, as her auntie forced the broom handle down the toilet once again, forcing all the water to turn brown, and cursed in Polish:

"Oh, what a stubborn turd!"

Her father was far more pragmatic, and whilst he pulled a face, that suggested he wasn't totally at ease, standing in the stench-filled room, or that his daughter was seeing a bloke who smelled like a slurry truck, patted me on the back and said: "These things happen."

Or put it another way – SHIT HAPPENS!

The Lord works in mysterious Poos

While working my way around the world, I stayed for several months picking various fruit on the Greek mainland.

During a particularly lean period, I was forced into the mountains of the Northern Peloponnese to pick grapes, like an elephant searching for water in Etosha National park, having to travel hundreds of miles to make ends meet.

The village we stayed in was tiny and had very limited accommodation, so during the grape-picking season the village priest was asked to put workers up at the local monastery.

Migrant workers slept in the aisle of the Monastery in sleeping bags. I happened to be one of them.

After putting in a particularly impressive shift, a beaming Greek farmer, who had taken a shine to me, asked me to come for supper at his 'speti'. His wife had made a rather tasty potato and steak meal, which had been soaked in an alarmingly excessive amount of olive oil. Though scrumptious, I knew the amount of olive oil I was digesting would cause trouble. Could I afford the laundry bill?

It was a brief thought that would come back to haunt me several hours later, rendering me out of the game for two or three days.

The night had gone well considering I didn't speak Greek, and he spoke only broken English. At one point we both roared with laughter after he said something to me that I didn't understand, and I replied by saying "What do you mean your wife wears no knickers" He didn't understand either, but smiled and raised his glass to me and downed in one an extremely large mug of homemade retsina.

I was not man enough to do the same but sipped my glass over a period of about two hours, just before the ouzo appeared. That's when I knew I was in for a bad night and would spend it in trap two.

As I settled into my sleeping bag for the night, the pain started, and as the hours passed, the pain got more intense, and shifted lower down. I waited as long as I could until I couldn't hold it in anymore. The last shooting pain dropped the bulk of the olive oil-soaked steak into 'the loading bay'.

I struggled with the zip of my sleeping bag in a desperate attempt to get out of it. As I hurtled down the aisle, buttocks clenched, and sweating profusely, I knew I wouldn't make it. I managed to get to the door but no further. Squatting down, I desecrated the steps of this holy place with a mixture of relief and shame.

I was squatting on the steps for ages, so much so, if a local had passed, they'd have thought I was a newly carved statue, a sentinel guarding the gates of heaven. It was never-ending, I didn't realize one person could crap so much, it was exhausting, I must have lost several pounds in weight and most of my dignity.

When I had finished, the steps were in a terrible state, as was my sphincter - swollen like a blood orange. I realized with some concern, that I didn't have any toilet paper. Indeed, the Greek equivalent of Andrex didn't produce enough tonnage of toilet tissue to clean up my messy arse.

How embarrassing to be left like a puppy sitting next to its spending. I was dressed in my shorts and only had my money belt. Deciding not to rip some pages out of my passport was one of the best decisions I've ever made. Opting for the only possible solution to my dilemma, I took my shorts off and used them as best I could, to clean myself up.

Not a very good job I might add, especially in the moonlight. It was like the cleanup of the Exxon Valdez.

I didn't know what to do with my badly soiled shorts; I certainly couldn't put them back on, that would be social suicide, a fashion *faux pas*. Then like the blinding light that knocked St Paul off his horse on the road to Damascus, it came to me, I would throw them on the monastery roof. I couldn't possibly throw them as far as the main monastery roof. However, there was a porch area at the front, which could be the final resting place for my now-defunct shorts.

I threw them up as far as I could, and they landed out of sight on the sloping vestibule.

Due to the trauma and sickness, I was drained and went back into the monastery to sleep before starting work. Exhausted and too weak from the previous night's ordeal, I was unable to wake at six o clock to leave for work with the other grape pickers.

I failed to warn them of the catastrophic sight that they would be greeted with upon opening the main door. To my horror, a Scottish lad was first out in the watery autumnal sunshine.

He was aghast at the carnage left on the steps, and shouted, "Christ lads, a donkey been in the night and shat on the steps. Good god, you'd think the farmer would tether it." I didn't have the nerve to mention I'd done it.

Later in the day, he said "The strange thing about that donkey shite business, It didn't have any hay in it". You didn't have to be David Attenborough to figure that it was a waste of humankind, but like the coward I am, I pretended to be surprised and muted comments like "REALLY" and "HOW ODD".

Some days later, having been well enough to go to work - I was walking back with the others to the monastery when we noticed the priest up on the roof. He never said anything about my shorts, but a day later we were all asked to leave the village under a cloud. To this day the others are bemused by the way the whole village's attitude towards us suddenly turned.

My lips are sealed of course, unlike my bottom on that occasion.

The language of LVIV

The food in Ukraine is rather odd for a Western European palate: pork fat covered with chocolate is just one example.

On arrival in Lviv after a very long train journey from Warszawa, I was starving and needing sustenance. Not knowing where to eat, I stumbled upon a small café style eatery, which served what looked like traditional Ukrainian fare. That was the problem, Ukrainian fare. Salted pork fat dipped in chocolate may be like an elephant seal to a Great White in these parts, but to a Western palate, it spelled a serious trip to the toilet at best, and a change of underwear.

Now I admit, I did have a few beers the night before, just to help me sleep you understand. The problem was it was the main road, and I had terrible trouble trying to fully close the window. The traffic noise from the street below was like the shelling of a Beirut suburb. One of the hinges had come off and the rest of the window was held in place with little more than fishing wire and chewing gum.

I woke the next morning with a slight hangover. The sunlight was blindingly bright, due to the threadbare nature of the cheap, but not remotely cheerful curtains. Completely naked, I got out of bed and went to the window, to have a look at Lviv in daylight. The evening before, it had resembled a Wild West frontier town, and I was keen to see it in all its glory. Lviv on the other hand was not ready to see me in all my glory.

The old net curtains covered my embarrassment, but as I peered out, a sudden urge to pass wind came over me. What followed was particularly upsetting, and I was relieved the net curtains had seen better days.

I don't often do it, indeed, I pride myself on never having stains in my underpants, but on this occasion, as I farted, I followed through. Technically, a different animal, the medical term for it is 'shart'. The 'shart' is a common complaint amongst children under the age of four, and 'wino's' over thirty.

The problem being it squirted onto the net curtains. I was appalled, as I'd never soiled myself in such a way before.

It was not a particularly bad stain, but it smelled too high heaven. How would I feel, or should I say, how would the cleaner feel, when she entered the room and was confronted with such a ripe-smelling gravy stain?

There was only one thing for it, apart from setting fire to the net curtains, which may land me in jail or hospital, or jumping to my impending death, equally unacceptable ends to my, as yet unfulfilled life I would have to mask the smell with a cunning plan.

I made myself a coffee to ponder my options. Then I had a light bulb eureka moment whilst holding my cup. That was it: the coffee. I used the last remnants of coffee from the sachet to rub over the offending stain. Pleased with my handy work, I bent down and quickly sniffed the new coffee stain for authenticity. Whilst not the comfortable and welcoming aroma of a newly opened jar of Nescafe - I think I got away with it!

I ate at McDonald's for the remainder of my trip. Better safe than sorry.

Drop your guts

In the spring of 1986, after a considerable length of time spent working 77 hours a week in the mountains of Nepal for the princely sum of $US2 per week, that's right $US2 a week, not an hour. Believe me, it was hard to motivate myself knowing I would receive a big fat nothing at the end of every week.

So, I talked myself out of taking on a career as a Nepalese waiter. It lasted about four months. After four months of living solely on curried lentils and rice three times a day, I feared that if my western palate was subjected to any more of this bland diet, it may well kill me off, or have a long-term effect on my health. Under my arms smelled of an odd mix of curried lentils and body odour, nothing could mask it: spraying myself head to toe in that very masculine fragrance *Hi Karate* made it worse.

It was very warm in the restaurant and the kitchens were unbearably hot. Unlike the food, which was quite often stone cold. Again, how do you motivate a chef that earns $3 a week, and sleeps under the tables in the restaurant, when everyone locks up and goes home? His whole life was stuffed into two plastic carrier bags, his worldly possessions hidden underneath a leaking sink unit.

I'd already had cholera and giardia, but I'll leave cholera for another story. Suffice it to say the effects of giardia: an amoebic disorder that covers your stools in a mucus membrane, and renders your bowels uncontrollable for weeks on end, with the socially unacceptable result of senseless farting, that smelled so obnoxious, when you let rip, you could cut the air with a knife.

After flying in from Bombay, my giardia was so severe, that when I broke wind in Northampton upon my return to England, I managed, with a mixed sense of shame and pride in equal measure, to clear a 24 full-size table snooker hall, quicker than an escaped tiger at Chester zoo. People ran for their lives.

The room was still empty twenty minutes after I'd the misfortune to 'drop my guts'. Indeed, the snooker hall manager was quite annoyed about it, asked for my membership card, and in a fit of rage, tore it up in front of me, saying I was to be given a lifetime ban.

A national first - barred for impersonating a skunk.

Suffering a second bought of uncontrollable flatulence, I passed wind in the lobby on my way out, just for good measure. That'll teach him I thought. The doorman said with menace "Drop your guts again mate and I'll drop you!

Like a skunk, I scurried away.

The air hung heavy, like the smog over Athens, when you leave the port of Piraeus. The smell clung to every fibre of my ill-fitting trousers; after all, I had lost nearly two stone in weight. I was beginning to become a social misfit. Everywhere I went I would break wind, and trade around the pubs of Northampton started to suffer as a result.

Even my friends stopped asking me out for a pint, they said my farts curdled the beer and that their partners could smell flatulence on their clothes when they got home, just like cigarette smoke used to linger after a night in the pub.

One couple broke up over my smell. He found it amusing, but she found it disgusting, they started arguing about him being very childish, the next thing she puts two fingers up to him and walked off shouting: "you were rubbish in bed anyway!!"

So it was thanks to my mum for making the appointment with the doctor, as my trumping had started to peel the wallpaper off the walls, and her kitchen cabinets started to fall off their hinges, I had put any medical consultation on hold, indeed my life was on hold, as I couldn't go out, and my mum could not invite any neighbours into the now shabby kitchen.

Seeking medical advice, the doctor mouthed the words "Phew - Good Lord!!!" on asking me to reproduce the fetid smell for him to diagnose, which to be honest didn't take long, it only took him one bite of the cherry.

He jumped to the conclusion, that my flatulence was like the winds up in Shetland; wild and unrelenting, and put me, rather swiftly, on a course of Flagyl tablets, and showed me the door.

He asked his secretary to hold all appointments for fifteen minutes whilst he opened the window and left the room himself.

These tablets were fantastic, extremely potent and cleared up the amoebic disorder in several weeks, and rendered my bowel inoperable for several days.

 The bottle boasted could dry up Lake Winnipeg. After taking them for a day or two, I would not doubt it!

It was like passing a medicine ball, nothing came out for days, even a fart, it was as though someone had smeared epoxy resin across my bum hole and let it set, but on the plus side, the air quality around Northampton cleared sufficiently to allow air traffic control to reinstate flights into Luton airport.

Land of the midnight flatulence

On a recent trip to Iceland, I happened to be flicking through the TV channels, after all, 23 hours of daylight means you have time on your hands, and there is only so much puffin you can eat or whales you can watch.

As Mr. Mannering commented in an episode of *Dad's Army*, in which the platoon was impressed that he could play the bagpipes when asked where he'd learned, he replied dryly "On my honeymoon in Scotland – the days were long but the nights were even longer."

I was only mildly interested in the Russian Eurovision entry, of four Russian women of indeterminable age, but certainly with a combined age of nearing five hundred years. My interest waned, however, when the Serbian entry began to warble like a song thrush in his mother tongue.

I turned to channel seven, which was showing a Rick Moranis hit comedy, in English with Icelandic subtitles, which I realized after a few dull minutes, would have been funnier if it had been in Icelandic with no subtitles The fact it starred Rick Moranis neither qualified it as a hit nor comedy.

By far the most entertaining channel was an episode, in English of *Embarrassing Bodies*. The whole half hour was devoted to flatulence. It caught my interest immediately. The television crew surveyed ten thousand people, and remarkably three percent said they had never farted in their lives, presumably, these three percent had been women, and probably religious.

According to the survey, people pass wind somewhere between ten and fifteen times a day. However, the most alarming statistic, which made me put down my Great Auk sandwich, was that anyone dropping their guts more than twenty-five times a day had bowel issues and should seek immediate consultation with a doctor. I noted with curiosity that there was no statistic for people who pass wind twenty times an hour. Presumably, if they had bothered to quote those formidable stats, the advice given would be, "Run for the hills."

So armed with my newly acquired data, I decided to survey myself, and I would count how many times I passed the wind. After two days I was slightly deflated and ashamed, a dismal tally, of trumping only eighteen times on both days. That did not include any seepage during sleep. Like evaporation from the Persian Gulf, the loss is incalculable.

The criteria for what passed as a 'trump' had me howling. Tears streamed down my face, as they explained that two or three trumps in quick succession, like an escaped convict playing percussion in an orchestra, only counted as 'one wind movement.'

It also went on to describe how pigeons escaping from a cardboard box just before an evacuation did not count at all.

Nevertheless, just eighteen was a poor show. I decided - like my school report had said at the end of most terms: "I must try harder". I would try again, but this time, I would eat a whole bag of dried apricots. I'm normally quite 'windy' after just a handful, but after a whole packet, it was a remarkable transformation, from Beaufort scale three a gentle breeze to force twelve; a hurricane.

My lower bowel ran like a racing car after a prolonged pit stop.

Just four hours into my 'fart-than I had passed the benchmark of twenty-five. At the end of the day, like a Buddhist prayer flag flapping on the slopes of Everest base camp, my sphincter was in tatters. Clocking up a mind-boggling fifty-nine, almost as much as a vegan can produce, on a diet of mung bean salad and soya milk.

I was certainly up there with farmyard livestock as a major contributor to the melting of the Polar ice caps. But, at that moment CO2 emissions and political correctness, were the last things on my mind. I was content, as relaxed in spirit as my sphincter was. As I climbed into bed at the end of such a momentous day, I squeezed out number sixty, lay on my pillow, and smiled with pride – reaching for the tube of *Anusol.*

The sunlight still glared through the window, although the hour was late, nearly 11:30 at night, thank god for the long hours, in the land of midnight flatulence.

"Where're my trousers?"

After a particularly heavy night on the beer in Alexandroupolis, it was with clenched cheeks that we boarded the train bound for Istanbul.

The last ouzo chaser the night before - whilst arm wrestling a local welder for one last beer had seemed a good idea at the time, but now seemed nothing short of greedy. Although the sun was shining and I was looking forward to arriving in Istanbul - a place I'd wanted to visit since watching *'Midnight Express'* the rumblings in my stomach, was not a good omen!

My companion had been drinking slightly more ouzo than me, he looked rather uncomfortable, but in a reflective mood, as he lifted his heavy rucksack onto his shoulder. Relieved that the strain had been safely dealt with, we boarded the train and started to look for a spare carriage with two empty seats. It was July and crowded with holidaymakers, although not many Greeks. As we know the Greeks refuse to acknowledge that Turkey exists.

We passed several carriages until we found a suitable resting place, with two empty seats.

Miguel lifted his rucksack onto the luggage racks above our heads, with little difficulty. After all, he was 6ft 2 inches. I asked him if he could put mine up on the rack with his. Unfortunately, unprepared for the additional weight of our camping equipment, he shocked the six other people in the carriage: including a pregnant lady and a small impressionable child, as he farted under the strain. There was a deathly silence, and then a look from Miguel that will haunt me to my dying day: He bit his lip and rolled his eyes, as he had evidently 'sharted'. Wearing no underpants the stain expanded into the fabric of his khaki trousers, like a plague of locusts devouring a field of corn.

He backed out of the carriage and slithered away to the nearest toilet.

Some considerable time later, I caught a glimpse of him frantically trying to attract my attention. At this point, I noticed he wasn't wearing any pants and was desperately trying to cover his 'tackle' with a T-shirt, two sizes too small.

I ran out of the carriage to ask him what was going on. He started his sorry tale and began to laugh. In the toilet washing his trousers, he realized that they would take ages to dry, and hit on a brain wave: He noticed that the toilet window was open and thought if he held them out of the window, with the warm summer air and a speeding train, they would be dry in no time at all. He was right, they would. But.....

As he held on to his Sunday best, he did not contemplate that a train doing equally high speed may be going in the opposite direction. The force of the two passing trains known as the Doppler Effect, causing a swirling mass of air, pulled the waistband from his grip and launched his trousers into the Greek undergrowth, never to be seen again.

He asked if I could lend him a pair of shorts until we arrived in Istanbul. How could I refuse? Indeed, I was only 5 ft 7 and Miguel being 6 ft 2 meant he would certainly launch the myth in Istanbul at least, that all Englishmen were hung like 'Grand National winners', as he stepped off the train wearing bright red shorts that were five sizes too small.

"And how would you like that wrapped Sir?"

When I left school I went to work for a rather exclusive kitchen and bathroom showroom in Northampton, as a trainee designer.

The company was very proud of its rich clientele and the salesmen boasted in the privacy of the office at the size of the sales they generated individually, and the bonuses they received.

On Saturday, a bathroom salesman showed a young couple with a child around the showroom. At one point the child was left to wander on his own, whilst the salesman bestowed the virtues of gold finished, half-flush option on a Royal Doulton suite.

It is obvious now, what happened and where the young boy had disappeared. But the frantic search for the child backfired on the supercilious salesman, as he did not have time to check all the bathrooms were pristine, before the Arab delegation's imminent arrival.

Later that day, the bathroom manager looking red-faced and flustered opened the door to the showroom to his Middle Eastern client coming in from Bedfordshire, to choose a new bathroom for his newly converted barn.

He didn't usually show people around, but on this occasion decided he would be heavily involved in the sale, as he had a very high opinion of himself, that did not last more than that very afternoon.

As he got to the most expensive bathroom range in the showroom, he turned to the Arab, and with a great deal of pride stated: "And of course, this sir is our Jacob Delefon suite, the top of the range."

Smiling, he lifted the toilet seat and said: "Just look at the quality of that." To his horror, he peered into the toilet to find a steaming turd staring up at them both. The Arab frowned and his driver smirked and sarcastically mouthed, to the open-jawed salesman whether the turd was included in the price.

The child had thought the display was a real bathroom, with a fully functioning plumbing system, and had decided to use the toilet as it had been intended.

Needless to say, he did not get the sale, and to make matters worse, his senior manager made him remove the offending turkey with a pair of *Marigolds*, and clean around the bowl with Jiff and a toothbrush.

From that day on the term 'Dirty Arab' had a completely new meaning in the bathroom department.

The salesman was demoted and started to come to work unshaven with his shirts badly creased, with a slight smell of stale alcohol on his breath. His sales plummeted and the last I heard, had been given his marching orders.

Many years later, it turns out he got badly in debt, lost his house and wife, and was last seen living in a shop doorway and sleeping in a "wee wee" stained sleeping bag.

The moral of the story – Always check behind you after you flush. It could spell curtains for your career.

A Good Jobbie

Some time ago I decided I needed a change of scenery regarding my career. So, I joined an agency to see what might turn up.

After several telephone interviews, I found myself in the reception of a famous multinational bank in Cheshire - waiting to be interviewed for a job in IT. As suspected, the pre-interview nerves, coupled with two strong cups of coffee, and the fact that on that particular morning - in my haste to avoid rush hour traffic - I hadn't actually 'gone', culminated in me wanting to 'go'.

Sitting at the reception desk were two extremely attractive pneumatic twenty-somethings. I was desperate to go to the toilet and worried about my impending interview.

I made a subconscious note that the GENTS were immediate to the left of the reception desk.

I had twenty minutes to wait until my interview and thought that would be sufficient time to 'go'. So, taking the bull by the horns, I 'went', quicker than I thought, although, at the time I noted, it was a little bit 'whiffy', to say the least.

The girls in reception knew where I was, and why, but it was slightly embarrassing to think I would have to go back out and sit opposite them. I would have settled for that, in the same way, England would settle, for a draw against Spain in a football tournament, before the kickoff.

Kick-off it most definitely did!!! In the main reception, soon after I'd locked the door and dropped my trousers around my ankles.

I finished performing and mercifully noticed that the toilet had an extractor fan. I pulled the string of what I thought was the extractor fan, but to my abject horror, trousers around my ankles, I'd pulled the chord of the emergency alarm.

The noise was deafening, and to make matters worse - made no difference to the 'whiff' in the room. A crowd gathered by the door thinking I was in some need of medical assistance. Now everyone in the building had been alerted to my homemade 'emanation'.

The only assistance I required now was a ladder, to climb out of the window - run across the car park, get back into my car, and drive as fast as I could, back to Liverpool. Failing that, I could follow my turd into the toilet and escape, like Tim Robbins in The Shawshank Redemption.

A sense of resignation to the imminent embarrassing low I would face crept over me, as I speedily pulled my pants up, I heard the two girls in reception saying: "Is anyone in there? Are you going to be okay?" Unfortunately, I wasn't, far from it. I wanted to end my life right there, if I had a gun, I would have shot myself, twice for good measure.

I heard a voice from within say meekly: "Yes I'm ok."

The next sentence was the one I'd feared most: "Let us in, we need to disable the alarm."

Let them in I thought, I wouldn't let my worst enemy in at that moment, to this ungodly bouquet. It was at that point that my legs buckled.

I slumped down on the toilet, leaned forward, and with an extremely heavy heart, and empty bowel opened the door.

The look of disgust on their two faces as they entered the 'throne' room was one of utter revulsion, as the smell hit them, head-on, like a punch from Mike Tyson.

One of the girls looked me right in the eye and shook her head. I lowered my eyes and shook mine too, but for a completely different reason.

The braver of the two girls gave an audible "phew" and started to fiddle above my head with the alarm.

Thank the Lord - the alarm stopped. They both then looked at each other, as Mike Tyson gave another hammer blow, but this time the punch in the face was aimed in my direction. They both sniggered and went back to the reception desk. I trundled out like a sad abused cat, to a room full of extremely stern faces. I sat down bowed my head, and like a criminal at the gallows, awaiting my sentence.

I looked up occasionally to see the two girls looking in my general direction. They appeared to frown in a belittling manner. The sniggering continued, and that look – like I was something they had stepped in – to be honest, the toilet did smell like something they had stepped in, and probably would until midmorning. I wanted the ground to open up before me, and take me to a less painful place. Burning in hell would have hurt less.

 I never found out if it was my lack of IT expertise, or the fact I had 'thrown the towel in' before the interview started, but I never got the job, and thankfully I don't bank there either. I am happy to give it a wide berth, so our paths will never cross, unlike the two chords in the toilet.

Since then, No matter how smelly the aftermath of a bowel movement is, If I have to go in a public toilet, I don't under any circumstances activate the extractor fan. If someone is waiting outside, then it is far less embarrassing to own up, hands aloft, and say to them: "Sorry that one is a bit ripe, I'd wait 5 minutes if I were you mate".

Jobbie Done!

Chinese Poo??

Polish people are quite odd. I should know - I married one. My wife went through many health fads, and at a drunken New Year's Eve party, I was waiting for the bathroom, and accidentally walked in on her. I was greeted by the sight of her drinking her urine. Believe it or not, drinking your own 'aqua vita' is beneficial to the immune system.

The only thing it made me immune to, was kissing her at the stroke of midnight. I had noticed a slightly nasty aroma earlier in the night when I had been talking to her, but I put it down to the schnapps we were drinking. The smell was particularly unpleasant. Not dissimilar to walking down a back alley and finding a disused sleeping bag, that belonged to a tramp with prostate issues. She asked me why I pulled a face! She thought I was the odd one. I ask you!!

I never tried it myself, the bladder cocktail, but my wife and her mother swore by it. I in turn, just swore at them for doing it. But I would say that, wouldn't I?

Allegedly the first of the day is particularly rich in minerals and nutrients, when the urine is so yellow it is almost brown. In olive oil terms, that would be the 'cold pressed' or 'first pressing'.

It was on one morning after a quick kiss I commented on her fetid breath and told her to do something about it, or a divorce was imminent. As it happens, unbeknown to me at the time, a divorce was imminent, but due to her running off with an Italian colleague from IBM, not due to the diabolical fumes steaming off her. Perhaps that was how she lured him! The gargling -'wee wee' siren.

Anyway - I haven't eaten *Spaghetti Bolognaise* since!

We got into a quite heated debate, about the virtues of drinking 'your piss', and she told me that lots of celebrities drink their brew. I asked her to name one; the only one she could come up with was Sarah Miles. Hardly a celebrity these days, and regardless of her celebrity status, she is well known in Hollywood as 'barking mad'. I retorted, rather sarcastically: "Sarah Miles - Oh well, that's all right then. Let's all start drinking our own homemade brew."

Anyway, as she was eulogizing about the famous people who bestow the virtues of carrying out such a socially unacceptable act, She said, "…And you know, the Chinese Prime Minister…"

She paused at this point, and I replied after a few seconds, "Eats Poo?" She replied: "Oh - I don't know his name!"

As you can imagine I roared with laughter.

The Goan Pigs

Whilst traveling on an extremely tight budget in Goa, and by tight I mean $5 a day, I needed somewhere to rest my weary head.

As you can imagine my choice of accommodation was a little limited. I had thought about sleeping on Colva beach, a picture-perfect vista by day, but at night, rabid dogs patrolled the shoreline, and incessant barking, would have kept Rip Van Winkle awake.

The best chance of me getting a good eight-hour sleep was to ask a local fisherman if I could hire a room in his house. Mr. Rodriquez was a very jolly, plump chap. He was extremely dark.

Wearing little more than a handkerchief for a loincloth, it hardly covered a postage stamp, never mind his privates, which, from where I was standing, were extremely public. He had nothing to cover his embarrassment, so there was no chance of him covering his enormous 'behind'.

At one point he bent down, and the ambient temperature of the whole region dropped by two degrees, as his enormous rump cast Western India into the shade. However, there was one big plus about Mr. Rodriquez: He wanted to improve his English and didn't appear to understand the concept of money.

There are tribes in the Amazon with more fiscal acumen than Mr. Rodriquez. So, for the princely sum of $2 a day, I had a beachfront room in one of the world's most splendid paradises. What is more, he had moved himself and his wife out, to sleep on the veranda, whilst I slept in his bed. His bedroom was a generic term, as the furniture had seen better days. Indeed, the room was so untidy, and it looked like it had taken the brunt of a recent cyclone. Still, I was safe in the knowledge that if a tsunami hit in the night, nothing would get passed that fat arse of his.

He also insisted on letting me eat with the family, for free. This bloke would have given Conrad Hilton a run for his money, Asian entrepreneur of the year.

Though free, the food was a little bland. Fish, followed by fish, washed down with more fish! They did have some rice and fruit and vegetables came in the guise of star fruit off the tree with an occasional coconut and mango.

I dropped the occasional mango and coconut myself. It was difficult not to in India. Everyone ends up with 'the runs'. It is inevitable as paying taxes and dying. No one escapes, not even the Indians.

The cost was a huge plus to staying with Mr. Rodriquez. There was a downside, that being no toilet. In a land where you are more likely to get the 'squitters' than a suntan, it was a dilemma.

It is hard to believe that in Goa, where the sun shines constantly for six months, at an equitable 32C - it would be difficult not to get a tan, but, it is probably as a result of spending so much time in the *'Karsie'*.

Tourists - come back from India, looking like they have spent the last six years in solitary confinement, in a POW camp.

They come back as white as a Beluga whale and feeling, probably looking like, a recently dug-up corpse.

I asked him where the toilet was, but his Portu-English was awful, and he resorted to a bizarre mime, which was like watching a rude game of charades after the 9 pm watershed. He kept squatting down only for his left testicle to pop out. He would smile, reach into his ill-fitting loincloth, and put it back.

The top and bottom of it – an apt phrase, was that basically when they needed to go, they crapped in the forest.

He walked me about 100m from the house to a small mound, behind which were lots of smaller mounds of humankind. On top of this mound of earth - covered with flies and biting ants - was a broken drainpipe precariously perched, and slanting downward towards a rancid pit of poo?

For privacy, his long-suffering wife had woven a panel out of banana leaves. It was stuck in the ground, shielding the view from the house, but on the three other sides, you were performing feral. Open to the elements.

To make matters worse there was no toilet paper. Instead, there was an old tin full of brown water, with which the incumbent squatter-cleaned themselves using their left hand. In ancient Rome, they were more civilized!

Earlier in the day, I caused quite a stir, by dipping into the communal rice bowl at lunchtime with my left hand. A culinary 'no no',

Upon my first trip to the toilet, I could not believe what happened. I wandered into the forest in the general direction of the banana panel. Suddenly a group of wild pigs came running from the trees. I nearly filled my pants in fright. They ran past me making excited pig noises and gathered around the earth mound at the bottom of the ordure-filled cesspit.

 They jockeyed for position, as I gingerly perched my bare behind on the drainpipe. At this point, the thought of people watching me was far from my mind. I was more worried about the pigs, and possibly falling backward into my feculence.

As I forced one out with ease - too much breadfruit and mango - I suspected - I heard squabbling behind me. The pigs were fighting over my shite. The biggest pig won the battle. As I looked down in horror, he looked up at me, with a hint of admiration. He had a little bit of poo on the end of his nose, and, as I looked away, the sunlight caught his eye, and he appeared to wink at me as if to say, "Thanks a lot".

He grunted in euphoric gratitude, as I had grunted in euphoric gratitude for ridding myself of the starfruit, without slipping into the hell hole of human waste, only moments earlier.

Buses always come in Number Two's

By far the most uncomfortable feeling anyone can have, apart from - accidentally meeting your lover with her husband at the checkout - is being desperate to take a dump and having to hang on. Forget bursting for a piss - for some reason, whilst that is certainly uncomfortable, and if you wait long enough quite painful - it doesn't come close.

But, and like Clarissa Dixon Wright, it's a big butt, the rewards when you finally unload are almost orgasmic. The agony and the ecstasy I call it. Nothing brings on a blind panic more than hanging on to a 'turtle head' when you know you are a long way from the nearest toilet, well, perhaps losing your passport at check-in, but not much else.

If you asked Stephen Hawking what ten multiplied by ten is if he needed to take a dump, he would be incapable of telling you - his mind is as empty as a goldfish. Forget black holes, the only hole he'd be interested in at that particular moment would be his arse hole.

 For some reason, the urgent need to empty one's bowels, can manifest into primeval uncontrollable twitching, and squirming that happen under no other circumstance. Rather like a temporary bout of Tourette's Syndrome.

For a start, you physically start to sweat. Everywhere! It can be minus 27C in the Yukon; Polar bears can be fighting on an ice flow, but the prospect of 'soiling yourself', brings you out in a heat rash.

Once it is in the 'loading bay' and the bomb doors have been activated, not even running to the toilet helps. Indeed, by an awful quirk of nature, rushing to the toilet is the worst thing you can do. It is human nature, at the 'target locked' stage - the point of no return - to walk in slow motion to avoid a premature trip to the laundrette.

On one such occasion, in Calcutta; where everyone barring locals, are in a perpetual state of 'Bomb bay' red alert: Like a caterpillar looking for leaves, the foreigner is always, on a constant vigil to find 'the bog'.

I was on a bus heading down the main thoroughfare - Chowringhee Street; I was just passing the Calcutta Museum near Sudder Street, so I knew it was ages until my hostel stop. Suddenly, the shooting pains started, I knew rice water wasn't far behind, I needed to evacuate, and IMMEDIATELY.

I didn't care where I was in a city of nine million, or that it would be a long wait for another bus all I cared about, was getting rid of last night's supper. I didn't care where, anywhere, except in the lining of the shorts   I was currently wearing.

The bell rang for the bus to stop, it may have only been one dull note, but it was music to my ears. Remember the TV series *Name That Tune* - "Well Tom, I'll name it in one." And as quickly as my tightly clenched buttocks would allow, I made my way to the front door.

I was so alarmed by my predicament that I didn't even wait for the bus to come to a complete standstill - it was still moving, and so was my arse. I jumped off, completely oblivious to the crowd gathered at the bus stop. I let out a joyous "Ahh" as I'd managed not to fill my freshly laundered shorts.

Sadly, my joy was short-lived as my own "Ahh Bisto" moment stopped several commuters in the tracks. The throng of people waiting to get on the already crowded bus was less than understanding. Unconcerned that I'd just done my business in front of them, yet agitated that I might make them late for work!

I was still in a squatting position when I looked up and caught the eye of a waiting nun, who was just in the process of straddling me to get on the bus.

I nodded and smiled from the filthy street where I deserved to be and said "Morning", she nodded knowingly as if she too had once been caught out in the cat-and-mouse game of undergarment Russian roulette. I had now joined the underclass, the untouchables. She knew it and I knew it.

Had no one got an ounce of shame left I thought? In particular, I had left dignity at the border crossing with East Bengal. Embarrassment spent, ring piece battered and bruised. The toilet roll is complete

In all my confusion and haste, I realized I had left my rucksack on the bus. My misery was complete. An arm appeared from the window, holding my rucksack. I stood up exposing my tackle to the rush hour traffic.

The bus had left, and I was left, humiliated, sitting in my excreta, tackle exposed, wondering how the hell I was going to wipe my bottom.

My life had hit a new low point as my tackle swung dangerously close to an open sewer, I wished at that moment, it had been my final resting place. I could be flushed away out of sight, out of mind.

Hearing a trumpet noise I turned around, looked up, and saw a portly man blowing his nose. He dropped the tissue on the floor next to me.

I thought shall I or shall I not, deciding on the latter, as a snot-filled tissue only gets you so far on the road to a clean crack.

King Juan Carlos meets Dracula

Food Glorious Food may have been a surprise hit from the early Seventies much-loved musical Oliver, but not in darkest, communist Romania in 1982.

Food, what food?

Ceausescu built the biggest palace of any potentate on the planet. I'm sure he boasted in meetings - with other leaders of the Warsaw Pact in dimly lit rooms behind the Iron Curtain - "Mine is bigger than yours". It was, he had to spend the national wealth of the nation on something, and it certainly wasn't on infrastructure or feeding his people. So, when you have spare billions in your current account, unaccounted for, why not get rid of it by building a huge pad for yourself?

I think they call it 'trousering'

Ceausescu's favorite Oliver was Fagin's hit: *You've Got To Pick A Pocket Or Two*. He took the advice literally - and stole money from everyone in Romania.

The shops in Bucharest in 1982 were completely bare. The only food I found in large quantities, were jars of pickled gherkins, bread, and tins of pilchards in tomato sauce. So unless you were a cat or the chief gherkin buyer for McDonald's, Romania wasn't the place to be wined and dined. Probably still isn't.

I can't abide pilchards in tomato sauce. The best thing - in my opinion - is to bypass the digestive tract, open the tin, and pour it straight down the toilet. Save time by cutting out the middleman.

There are two things I hate more than pickled gherkins: traffic jams and Mr. Bean cartoons, though Buster Keaton's silent films run him a close second. If I go to McDonald's, which is very infrequently, I have to remove the gherkin from my Big Mac. I don't see the point of them, they make me bilious, and to be honest, I'm windy enough without it coming out both ends.

So, for my week in Bucharest, I went on an involuntary hunger strike, in the land that was a culinary wasteland. No wonder Dracula started drinking blood. He couldn't find anything else to sink his teeth into. – That's a fact.

I was so hungry, at one point I considered eating my earwax or the fluff out of my belly button. I had heard that after a nuclear winter one of the only things to survive are cockroaches: They can survive for two years at the bottom of a linen basket, by eating dust.

Truth was, I was wasting away, like Bobby Sands during his 'dirty cell' protest. They say a man cannot live on bread alone, but as dull, and as stale as it was, I was forced to do so.

So... when a local on the tram was tucking into a chicken wing, and some kind of dough ball soaked in vodka, I started to drool like Clement Fraud's dog. I couldn't take my eyes off him. The drooling left an embarrassing damp patch in the crotch of my beige trousers. I looked like one of the cast members from *One Flew Over The Cuckoo's Nest*. He noticed me and my expanding wet patch, smiled, and offered me a piece of chicken and alcohol-soaked bread.

It was only after I'd eaten it, that I realized I should have stuck to pilchards in tomato sauce. The chicken was 'on the turn' and raw in places. If not raw, cold enough to suggest I would be in for a spot of 'trouble' later.

The vodka bread balls were far too strong for my delicate western palate, if indeed it was vodka, it tasted like paraffin.

Some hours later; you've guessed it, I found out, the chicken had indeed been raw, and it was, as I had expected had been paraffin. It certainly went through me like paraffin.

I found out that the Eastern Block, before 1990, used to pick their women's Olympic shot-putting team from a shoddily dressed bunch of Romanian toilet attendants.

The female attendant guarding the public toilets as vehemently as Cerberus, the three-headed hound guarding the gates of hell was no beauty. Even in porcine circles, the term lipstick on a pig would have been apt.

If Cerberus had been a nanosecond longer dispensing the bog roll, Bobby Sands would not have been the only one sitting in a dirty room.

My Romanian wasn't up to much, certainly not fluent, but I got the message, she was in no hurry to let me pass unless I crossed her paw with silver.

I was so close to the toilet, I had inadvertently 'relaxed', and being pinned up at the shit house door - by a person of indeterminate sex, with a grip of steel - did nothing to arrest my urge to 'spread the load'.

I was frantic, searching through my saliva-stained trousers with one hand, whilst gripping my sorry buttocks with the other. I couldn't hold out any longer, I screamed like a banshee "Let me go, can't you see I'm about to shit myself?" I did note that the floor had been recently mopped, and she may put me in a death choke, should I spoil it.

I threw two silver coins at her, but to be fair, I'd have happily parted company with a £50 note, just to feel free of the terrible burden I was temporarily carrying.

She accepted the coinage she smiled, so I knew I'd given her far too much, returning the favour, she unraveled her toilet roll and gave me what I considered was far too little. In fact, a single sheet of dire quality, the thinnest I'd ever seen. I'd blown bubbles of fairy liquid with thicker membranes.

Andrex it most certainly was not.

I looked at her in disgust, what good was that to anyone I thought, as I turned and gave it toes to the nearest cubicle.

As I 'pebble dashed' the pan, I pondered my predicament. How to make the best use, of a single sheet of toilet paper? Origami was not something I was particularly good at, but I doubt a Japanese expert could have made a 'flapping bird' out of a single sheet of Romanian bog paper.

I feared it was 'brown fingernail' time.

But wait, perhaps not.

I remembered in my rucksack, I had an old map of Spain. On one side, was the complete Iberian Peninsula, and on the other, was a photo of King Juan Carlos.

I will say, that by the time I had finished wiping, the motorway network through Spain had been hastily extended, and a new, extremely wide highway ran from Madrid past Barcelona, into what can only be described as land reclaimed from the Mediterranean.

On the other side of the map, most alarmingly, I had inadvertently given his majesty – King Juan Carlos of Spain, what is commonly known as, a 'dirty Sanchez'.

Flying by the Seat of your Pants

As 1985 drew to an inevitable close, and the world partied, at the stroke of midnight, I was in the toilet at Dhaka International airport, stroking my backside for the very last time that year. A minute later, I was still mercifully cleaning myself up for the very first time in 1986.

In an act - similar to crossing the *international date line,* in the middle of the Pacific - I had managed unintentionally, but no less impressively, in a small toilet cubicle in Bangladesh - to straddle a period of two years in a single movement. A bowel movement!

The poster in Rangoon's travel agents read:

"Fly Biman - The better you know Bangladesh"

This is a misleading statement and could be challenged in a court of law by any half-decent defamation lawyer, to be libel.

It should have read:

"Fly Biman – You should know better"

This would be nearer to the truth. We departed terra firma in Dhaka, in a fashion model to that of a Harrier Jump Jet, and seemed to glide into Calcutta. The pilot had the misfortune of flying the most unreliable aircraft engine in the Commonwealth.

Arriving in Calcutta - in the same style we had left Dhaka - on the back of an airborne 'Big Dipper ' – vertically - we fell onto the runway from what must have been a hundred feet. For a moment we were airborne again, and then the pilot, who I am sure had little more than an international driver's license, and was only in the captain's seat, due to winning an obscure Bengali television programme, along the same lines as our very own *Jim'll Fix It*, proceeded to impress everyone on board with his aerial tomfoolery - attempting a second landing on his front wheel.

He stopped a little too abruptly for everyone's liking, to a crescendo of blood-curdling screams, from the passengers, and more disturbingly the employees at Dum Dum Air traffic control tower, at the end of a 10,000ft runway, with only inches to spare.

The pilot was out of his depth and was forced to call for assistance to be towed in reverse to the terminal.

I am sure, the aircraft manufacturers McDonnell Douglas - would have been horrified at the man's blatant disregard for a superb piece of mechanical machinery. Just as certain, Evel Knievel would have taken his hat off to the man for his nerves of steel.

Turn Left at Biffins Bridge

Cycling is fun, but only if you live in Holland or on the Bolivian Salt Pan, and let's face it, only necessary if you are strapped for cash and can't afford either a motorbike or a car. It is at those moments in your life that you begin to recall your teacher's comment: To pay more attention in class. Well, guess what sunshine? It might have helped you get a better job later on in life, you waster!!!

No sight grates more than being piss wet through waiting for a bus when the school nerd drives past in his Bentley GT. Point taken!

I hadn't been on a bike in ten years. I wasn't sure I would still be able to find it in the garage, under the mountain of boxes of unwanted ornaments and old *Top Of The Pops* Volume 17 LPs I was hoarding in the garage. All teenage boys know the mysterious pelvic pleasure of finding 70's Top Of The Pops album covers at the bottom of your dad's HiFi cabinet. Everyone's personal pre-pubescent favourite: The *Gratton's* catalogue. Pages 71 –79 inclusive: Ignoring ladies dressing gowns and full corsets – Grandma style.

The bike in question was an extremely cheap mountain bike called KILIMANJARO. That was where the relationship between mountain and bike ended.

This particular mountain bike was so poorly constructed it had trouble getting over speed bumps, let alone going up hills.

I noticed that when I sat on it, I was a little close to the ground and that the wheels were a little small, and the tyres were too fat and chunky. Images of those horrible clowns at the circus, cycling along on tiny bikes to pre-recorded laughter, spring to mind. A pet hate of mine: Clowns.

I decided that the best thing to do - before my cross Britain dash - was to take it to the local bike shop for a service.

The shopkeeper was a sarcastic Scouser. As we all know, everyone born within the city limits of 'Scouseland' is by birth rite sarcastic, and proud of it. Anyway, this Liverpudlian could not help it, when he asked me "What is that, this is a bike shop?" I foolishly told him I was about to cycle across Britain on it.

The insidious nature of his banter toward me, was hurtful if accurately "spot on"

The subsequent high-pitched whistling noise coming out of his nostrils - as he tried to curtail a laugh - had dogs all over Anfield barking mad.

"Mate, Cycle across Britain? I wouldn't cycle to the shops on that". He added with an element of bemusement "That's a child's bike"!! I had thought, even to my vertically challenged stature, it was rather low.

He tried to convince me to part with 500 pounds on a new bike, but I thought, perhaps a little too abruptly "Sod it, I'll show him. I'm going on the KILIMANJARO". And stupidly I did.

I turned up at my mate's house unprepared.

Dressed in a Tony Hawkes skateboarding helmet, that had brought jeers from a crowd of 'no marks' hanging around a bus shelter. I had almost fallen off, when I narrowly avoided a parked car, as I attempted to turn and give the 'two fingered' salute to them, as they shouted "The kip of him".

As we set off, the others asked how much water I was carrying in my rucksack. They all had CAMELBAKS, I said "What water?" They asked, "So why is your rucksack so heavy"? They had gathered it weighed a lot, as every time I went around a bend, I leaned like Barry Sheen at *Silverstone*.

I opened it and showed them: A pack of Kendal mint cake, an economy-size bottle of Listerine mouthwash, and, a shoe polish brush. I can see you all shaking your head in collective disbelief.

We were cycling from Morecambe to Scarborough and it was going to take three days. Across the Pennines, with a chest infection, no water, but a lovely fresh feeling in my mouth, - the minty taste lasted all day. Unfortunately, I didn't.

The lack of hydration took its toll, and I fell behind after thirty miles. I was wobbling erratically, almost delirious.

I fell off after three miles when we stopped abruptly and I forgot to take my foot out of the pedal straps. Falling into a bramble bush, silently, like a cunning fox after a hare. I slid into a barbed wire fence. Cut to ribbons, stung by nettles, pinned to the fence, I crucified myself, as I somehow managed to get the barbed wire, stuck behind my ear. The rain came down like pencils, in a biblical torrent, my panniers snapped and I was forced to cycle the remaining 160 miles with it held in place with a piece of string. All in all, I was a sorry-looking sight.

By the end of day one, just out of Settle which was so steep I couldn't cycle more than a few metres without getting off and pushing the damn thing the next four miles, I was in a terrible state. My Tony Hawkes skateboard helmet looked like a disco ball there were so many dried sweat crystals embedded in it.

The sweat on my handlebars looked like a diamond-encrusted bicycle commissioned by car tuners/accessorizes - Mansory.

Every day, as I rubbed my extremely tender scrotum, my dad would phone to ask how it had gone and to ask my whereabouts. He had been monitoring our progress on the Internet, via an ordinance survey map.

By day three my 'Biffins Bridge' was in a right mess. My gel seat did little to ease the abject pain of every revolution of the wheel.

My arse, and particularly my sack, swelled up to an alarming, if somewhat, pleasing size. To be hung drawn and quartered would hurt less. 'Biffins' was weeping, and so was I, as we relentlessly pushed on.

Lord have mercy on my sorry sack.

I pedalled into Scarborough resembling a cast member of Schindler's List - Arsehole in tatters, my perineum weeping, like a teenager who had just been dumped by her first love.

The train journey home to Liverpool was a godsend - welcome relief. My bum had been through the trenches. I gingerly stepped off at Lime Street station and limped to the local platform, weary but triumphant. I couldn't face cycling home and roadside saddle, as the queen does. I might add riding side saddle was particularly difficult, I have a new respect for the equestrian skills shown by senior members of the Royal household.

When I got home my dad called and said: "Where the hell did you go? I followed you as far as Biffins Bridge and I couldn't find it anywhere. I have no idea where it is. Is it the other side of Bridlington?"

I told him it was closer than he thought.

When I told him what I meant when I said: "Day three is a lot easier, but Biffins Bridge is in a terrible mess", he laughed.

However, it was a good few weeks before I laughed again. My scrotum scabbed up something awful. And, for a month, I made a General Hogmanay Melchett-style "Oh ah" noise, every time I eased myself into a chair.

I haven't cycled since, but I am pleased to announce: Biffins Bridge made a full recovery.

Bored Shitless

Everyone knows what it is like to attend an extremely dull meeting, especially in IT, which seems to attract more than its fair share of very serious, earnest individuals. The sort of people you would not like to be set adrift in a lifeboat with.

Indeed, if I ever had the double misfortune of firstly crashing into the sea, and secondly, after surviving the impact, finding myself stuck in a small craft with a group of IT geeks, I would probably jump out and take my chances with the sharks, or wait until nightfall, and eat them one by one.

At one such 'workshop' the subject matter was Mainframe Encryption. A subject matter so dull and so complex, that Einstein once did a talk on it, and dozed off mid-sentence.

The room was full, there must have been twenty people sitting around the boardroom table, and only two people had a clue what was going on.

Looking around the room, I noticed everyone was nodding and smiling in the right places, but they were all thinking about their holiday entitlements or the burst water pipe at home. They certainly weren't thinking about the question at hand.

The bloke opposite me put his hands to his chin, as though he was praying, in a statement that said, "Let me consider that a moment", when I knew, and he knew that I knew, he was "bored shitless".

In truth, the same bloke told me the day before - that World War 2 ended in 1985!! So how he thought he could pull the wool over everyone's eyes - and have everyone in the room believe he knew about Mainframe Encryption, when in truth, he probably had trouble spelling it - is anyone's guess.

As one hour, dragged into two, time seemed to stand still, like a day on Venus. People started reading the words on the fire alarm. They started to take an interest in the air conditioning vents. They started counting the roof tiles on the ceiling. They gave no thought at all on the subject matter. It wasn't that they didn't want to know about Mainframe Encryption, they just couldn't grasp its complexity. It was like trying to teach quantum physics to a four-year-old

No one wanted to be there, and as the two-and-a-half-hour mark passed - without so much as a toilet break - fidgeting started. It was not worth clock watching, as when clock watching, the fingers never seemed to move. Like the clock tower in the memorial garden in *Hiroshima,* we were stuck in this meeting room for all eternity.

There seemed to be a lot of shifting in seats; doodling on notebooks; yawning uncontrollably, and that was just the bloke leading the meeting. To be honest, I had wanted the toilet for some time and had been shifting in my seat for a good hour and a half. People started to sneak the odd 'trouser cough', hoping everyone in the room would subconsciously blame the person sitting next to them.

So it was with genuine delight that the meeting was called to a close. And like a rat escaping from a playful cat, everyone scarpered, mostly into the 'gents'.

I was so keen to empty my rather full bowel, that I committed the cardinal sin - A restroom 'no-no'. I didn't check for toilet paper!

As a satisfyingly dull thud hit the pan, I turned to unravel the roll. To my horror, it was empty.

My dad always said: "Life is like a toilet roll, at first it goes around very slowly, but at the end, it whizzes around - far too quickly".

All that remained was the cardboard roll. I was stuck. My 'pollards' streaked the porcelain, and the last thing I needed was marble-effect underwear. I considered shuffling from one booth into another - trousers around my ankles - but knowing my luck, the IT Director would walk in.

I had an idea. I waited until everyone had gone out of the Gents, and then I phoned my mate with my mobile and explained my predicament. After he had stopped laughing, he obliged and I heard the Gent's door open, he walked over to the cubicle next to me.

He let out a slightly amusing, but genuine " Phwoar!!"

He said, "You owe me for this". Under the cubicle came the ultimate hand of friendship - he proceeded to hand me sheets of *Andrex* - one at a time, and to add to my embarrassment, waiting for me to wipe and beg for more.

As we left the toilet, he turned to me and said it sounded like a cat was doing its business in the cat litter...

Charming!!!!

Sorry, this page is blank as I had to stop to go to the toilet.

When you have got to go, you must go.

I mean be fair, you will stop reading this and do other things, so give me a break.

Right, I am back now, it was mundane and necessary.

I will carry on writing now.

Catastrophe avoided!

Set it Free

I do admire security guards. They have made a career out of doing absolutely nothing.

The only other people with more time on their hands are prisoners. So, how lazy are Prison guards? People with nothing to do, watching people, with even less to do.

You often see security guards, feet up, reading a very well-read newspaper. Or watching TV, eating chocolate digestives, sipping endless mugs of tea, and whispering into *walkie-talkies*: "Everything is okay here" Of course everything is OK. They only need a pair of pyjamas and they would be ready for bed.

But; Let me be frank. Face it - If there were no security guards, there would be an increase in crime, therefore, more prisoners, and an exponential increase in the number of prison guards – thus, an endless cycle of nothing. The way very clever scientists describe the eons before the 'Big Bang'.

When I arrived back from Australia, I needed a job. There was very little mainframe computer work, in 1992.

I went for an interview with that famous shipbuilder on the banks of the Mersey. To be honest, I didn't impress with the initial interview. When they asked how I would put out an electrical fire I suggested a water h!! I was very nervous, and meant t say foam, but that was wrong also.

I know the saying 'three strikes and out, but at the shipyard in those days, three strikes a week was normal. So, rather surprisingly, I got the job.

Next thing I know - I'm sitting in a porta-cabin on the basin wall - looking out over the Mersey - reading a newspaper, eating biscuits, and drinking gallons of tea. The shipyard was refitting a Royal Fleet Auxiliary ship, and my contract would last four months. After four months of gorging myself - I feared I'd end the contract looking like a walrus in a hard hat.

We designed a rota that meant we patrolled the 1,000 ft vessel constantly - mainly to stop us from overdosing on Kit Kats, and burn off the excessive number of calories we were consuming. Mountaineers climbing K2, consume fewer calories in a day. The ship was a hive of inactivity during the day, as everyone had union duties to attend to, but resembled the 'Marie Celeste' at night.

On one such night shift, I was patrolling the bow of the ship - near the Captain's quarters - when I was 'caught short. I knew it was a good ten minutes to walk off the ship and over to the security hut, so I made a tactical judgment: When you have got to go, you just have to go. I told my colleague - the biscuit-eating *pinniped* - to keep an eye out. There was no need - people crossing the Antarctic solo saw more people than us on board at night.

I went to the captain's 'Heads', and in the words of Captain Kirk: "The Captain's log, star date 1992 – Uranus"

As the Captain's log came into this world for the very first time, its life was cut short by cries from my colleague, alerting me to the fact this part of the ship, hadn't been plumbed in yet.

Merseyside had launched a host of famous vessels over the years. And now I was going to 'slide a brown' down the slips. How appropriate, that in this famous shipyard, I too, had launched my own 'floater'.

I looked behind me at my sorry stool, struggling in the waterless pit, like a lungfish caught between swampy ponds in the unforgiving African heat of the dry season. I knew there was only one thing for it.

I found a plastic bag and made a makeshift glove, scooping my helpless friend to safety from a perilous end. At that point the words of Rolf Harris came to me: "Did You Think I Would Leave You Dying "

I ran through the corridor, and as my colleague shouted after me: "That is one big turkey", with the unconditional love a father feels for his child, I reluctantly and a little tearfully, flung my 'spendings' over the side and into the river.

It was free, born free, as free - as the wind blows!

My Mersey Goldfish had a fighting chance. It may even return one day, like salmon around the globe, fighting against the strong eight-knot current, to breed in the murky waters of Birkenhead.

Red Alert!

For those with lycanthrope hairlines, a luxuriant head of hair can be a curse. Like a badger with fleas, you can end up looking remarkably unkempt. The Lord Mayor of London, Boris is a case in point. (When I first wrote this - Boris had not become Prime Minister, and I can say with certainty that he is not like a good bottle of claret, as has not aged well). He still looks like a badger's back.

From the neck down, you can tell he is 'rolling in cash, but sadly, from the neck up, he looks like he has been dragged through a hedge backward. No form of grooming can mask his disheveled appearance. That's what too much hair can do to a man.

I would say that of course, as I have very little of it myself - hair, or cash - for that matter!

So, whoever invented Brylcreem, I take my hat off to you. Some extremely rich people use the product, well perhaps not use it, advertise it, maybe more appropriate. As a result, they are handsomely rewarded for doing so.

I paid a very heavy price for using it. I suppose you could argue it was my fault. Foolhardy, some might say.

On the day I left to go around the world, I had the fiscal misfortune of changing my money when the dollars for pounds sterling reached a historic, all-time low. One pound bought just one dollar three cents. Donald Trump lookout, I'm behind you. There is another man whose hair lets him down; he may be a billionaire but you wouldn't give him a dime for that comb-over.

As a result, I didn't have much cash to play with and I hadn't even left our shores. To say I had to be frugal was an understatement. Buying stuff in *Pound Land* was as frivolous as eating truffles on a bed of saffron.

So, when a bloke in a pub told me a money-saving idea - to avoid buying expensive branded sun cream - I listened intently. It did sound feasible that the reason all taxi drivers appear to have very brown necks is due to the excessive Brylcreem they use in their hair. Funnily enough, I had noted that on a recent ride in a taxi, the driver had a neck George Hamilton III would die for.

That was my downfall, as I stepped out, onto the beach, on the Croatian Island of Brac, armed with little more than a snug-fitting pair of 'budgie smugglers' and my sun factor minus twenty, an economy tub of Brylcreem. I was asking for trouble. Who the hell wears budgie smugglers?

I can report, it went on beautifully smooth if a little greasy.

Twenty minutes of zero cloud cover in temperatures hovering around 35 degrees Celsius - I had started to notice a slight reddening around my shoulder, and five minutes later it became a tingle.

Half an hour later, I sensed a slight electrical burning smell in the wind but put it down to a man selling lamb kebabs close by.

When I woke up two hours later, I quickly realized, the burning smell had been me. Christ Almighty, I was blistering like a tar pit. Only the lord could save me now. Even my chest hair had singed.

The only place on my whole body, that didn't resemble a ripe, juicy plum tomato, was - oddly enough - my plums. I told you wearing "budgie smugglers" was a bright idea.

I burned like a witch on trial. The Kuwaiti oil fields generated less heat, when the Iraqis set fire to them, as they retreated over the border in 1990.

My nose, well, what nose? I looked like, a melting ice- cream cone, that a child had dropped on the pavement, on a particularly hot day.

I ran for the shade of a nearby umbrella, as my friend called for assistance. I shivered like a wet dog on top of *Helvellyn,* whilst the kebab seller called for an ambulance.

As the crowds dispersed, and the sun sank below the horizon, a glorious sunset was replaced by the rising moon. In a never-ending game of galactic billiards, I was emitting a strange luminous green hue - reminiscent of the meltdown in the core reactor of a nuclear power station.

Thinking the green light in the sky may be a rave – several people began to party.

The Great Escape

I had heard that women who live together, on occasion, fall in line with each other, in the cyclic ladies' department. But it is most unusual for blokes who share a flat, to want a crap at precisely the same time. It is even stranger, for them to have - a synchronized, ugly bout of diarrhea.

Like a referee and his assistant, attempting to synchronize watches at the start of a Premier League game - the drama unfolded!

We put it down to one of two things: A bad pint or two, or, more likely, the dodgy clam chowder we had eaten the night before.

I thought at the time, it wasn't the warmest soup I'd ever eaten, and sadly the clams were more like frozen prawns. The net result was, we had the trots on a campsite outside of Toronto. And 'trot' we did, back and forth to the campsite toilet block. On this occasion, we galloped like *Aldaniti* and arrived in unison.

Even though we were very good friends, pooing in public, is a touchy subject. There was an awkward pause as we looked at each other, hesitated, and nodded, as though a gladiator entering the arena. For most blokes, a good crap is a private affair - a LOVE affair - and the last thing you need is a gooseberry in the cubicle next door.

I chose trap one and he chose trap three. We left trap two empty. It was purely a psychological divide - an imaginary line, -like the tropic of Capricorn - it was only four feet, but it made a difference.

However, Four feet did not make the slightest difference to the acoustics. There was a 'Noah's Ark' of amusing animal noises, coming out of traps one and three. At one point it sounded like a bird of prey had flown through the open window, and my mate was having a fight with a Barn Owl, whilst trying to crap at the same time.

We did our best to deaden the sound. You know the drill: Toilet paper on top of the water; shift buttocks to left and right, so the offending 'Tommy' will hit the porcelain first and break its fall, so it slips silently into the murky water. Anything to stop the ultra-embarrassing SPLOSH noise we all hate. The aftermath which follows: Usually in the form of backwash - from the 'Barnes Wallace' bomb -which spills up and wets your arse, is always upsetting if always expected.

Every time I create an amusing SPLOSH, I bite my lip, and it was the same then. I bit my lip to stop myself from laughing.

A man came into the GENTS and seeing one and three occupied, he helped himself to trap two. The poor bloke must have had the same clam chowder as we'd eaten!

A whole lot of coughing, sniffing, and heavy breathing, and then he let out the god awful high pitched scream; not dissimilar to a soldier who has been shot, and is getting the lead shot pulled out of his chest with a pair of tweezers.

 He unleashed hell - Followed by a slight whimper - as though he was pining for something. After a slight pause came the lull before the storm. Bracing himself he prepared for the worse - Boy – it never rains, it pours! What came next can only be described as the opening scene from *Saving Private Ryan*. Absolute carnage!!

As he "oohed " and "aahed" we listened in quiet reverence, aware that we were witnessing something special, we were in the presence of ' thunder box' greatness. He was in the 'Throne room' Nirvana!! To us mere mortals he was a 'lavatorial god'.

We couldn't help ourselves. We burst out laughing!!

He shouted: "Hey – what's going on?" We laughed even louder. He then said: "Just wait till I wipe my arse, then I'll wipe the floor with you!"

With the threat of an imminent 'good hiding' hanging over us, we very swiftly, but not convincingly, wiped our arse and slipped silently out into the night, like our 'turtles head' had moments before.

Ride into Hell

I do accept that it was rather late when I arrived in Karachi, and the bus into the city had probably stopped running.

But to try and charge me thirty dollars - a man's wages for a month - did seem rather high. No matter how hard I tried to haggle with the blanket-clad rabble, I couldn't get them to drop the price. I was in a city of ten million, it was the other side of midnight - I hadn't a clue where I was, they had me over a barrel.

If I'd refused to pay they could have taken me down a side alley, and put me over a barrel. So, I reluctantly paid.

I climbed aboard the 'Tuk-Tuk', and a young impertinent local, slid in beside me.

He introduced himself. What the hell was he doing in my taxi? I placed my rucksack between us for good measure.

He began on a helpful note. He lived in Karachi, and he warned me there were a lot of bad people living in the city, that would want to take advantage of a westerner alone. He was at the top of my list of those people that might try.

He smiled a sinister 'Dick Dastardly' type smile. It sent a shiver down my spine. He praised himself as being an honest man and said that he would help me all he could, which was fine if I needed it, but I didn't. As I had suspected all along, he was the biggest cheat west of the Ganges Delta.

We arrived at an extremely low budget, well it can only be described as a hovel, but he called it a 'guesthouse'. The foyer was open to the street, and it had, without a shadow of a doubt been recently condemned. The rug hadn't seen a vacuum cleaner since *Ghengis Khan* rode through on his way to *Xanadu*. The cost of the room, was again, a rather convenient - thirty dollars. Thirty dollars could have bought the plot of land the hotel sat on.

This was supposed to be a budget trip. In the last hour, I was spending money like Heads of State. I did manage to talk the 'hotelier stroke slob' down to 25 dollars - if I stayed two nights. Take my bank details, empty my account - you heartless thieving git.

I was escorted to my open plan, by that I mean - open to the elements bedroom, by an overtly feminine-looking chap. These days I think they refer to them as *ladyboys*, but in 1986 I had never seen a '*chick with a dick*'. Still haven't, I might add. In those days *gay* meant happy, and the closest I'd been to a bloke who acted like my sister, was watching Dick Emery on Saturday nights.

I could hear my new taxi buddy babbling on in Urdu with the hotelier, no doubt negotiating a hefty commission.

Suddenly the biggest cheat in Pakistan came into my room, without so much as knocking - helped himself to the only chair, and poured himself a glass of water, with the familiarity of a husband and wife. He began to speak, and it was then that he made his motives clear. He made it sound as though, I was missing the chance of a lifetime. He would be my guide during my stay in Karachi, and he would haggle for me, look after me, and watch my back. I could throw in the meals, and all for fifty dollars. He didn't look like he had earned fifty dollars since the day he was born. At this suggestion; my face went a brilliant, flame red.

I was furious, the man's cheek, knew no bounds. I asked him to leave, but he just stood there. To make matters worse, a group had gathered at the door and started to giggle. He began with the cocksure attitude of OJ Simpson's attorney.

He started by saying I was an unreasonable man. He continued to slur my character by saying he had tried to bargain down the price of my taxi - when in truth - he was one of the ones who had tried to charge me thirty dollars in the first place!

The hard sell came next. He started a tearful tale and insisted I give him some cash, as his children were hungry, and one of them needed a life-saving operation. When I kept saying: "Bugger Off", he turned nasty, said I had wasted his time and that he should have stayed at the airport and waited for a plane full of Americans.

This was the final straw, as my already flame-red face turned an alarming puce. I yelled loudly and pinned him up against the wall. I said I'd rip his rudimentary 'testes' off if he didn't leave. He protested that he was a very poor man. I shouted it was better to be poor than crippled.

Sensing I'd had enough of him - and I might turn nasty myself - he left, Urdu expletives ringing in my ears.

Left alone in my room - surrounded by squalor - it was a good ten minutes before my face returned to its normal shade. Indeed, at one stage, I feared I would remain purple for good.

Terry Waite's Allotment

Whilst waiting for the second part of Monday night's *Coronation Street,* my girlfriend gave me the remote.

I started going through the programmes I had recorded on Sky Plus.

One of the programmes was Ross Kemp's *Extreme World.* I don't like him, but I like seeing him crap himself when interviewing hardened criminals in prison. He acts very toughly, but if it all kicked off, he would be first back to the safety of his on set caravan. He would wait until the coast was clear, and then, after a quick change of underwear, he'd be back out, the camera following his every move.

Ross Kemp was in Beirut in this particular episode, I was in Beirut in 2003, and it was a great place to visit. Everyone was really friendly, but the locals complained that nobody ever went there, mainly because, ten years after the fighting had finished, it still had the 'war torn' image.

I mean, ok, the buildings are pockmarked with bullet holes and parts of the city have not been rebuilt. But when I think about Pompeii, It is still a ruin, and Vesuvius has been dormant for centuries. You don't go on a day trip from Naples thinking you are going to be covered in a burning dust cloud. So why steer clear of Beirut?

My girlfriend was disinterested in the programme. She was more concerned about Deidre and Ken's marriage problems. However, to be fair, she sat through it, but with a face on her like a wet weekend.

Ross Kemp was in the area where Terry Waite was kidnapped, so I turned to her and said: "It must have been terrible", she said: "What was terrible?" I replied: "You know, Terry Waite was held in captivity for five years, in a room on his own, chained to a radiator ".

Her response was priceless. She turned to me and in a very serious voice said: "Was it on?" I said: "Was what on?" She said: "The radiator", in a voice that suggested I was the stupid one.

I couldn't believe it! I was slightly sarcastic with my retort, "How the hell do I know, to be honest, that would be the least of his problems".

She then said: "Well, I wouldn't be able to". I said in disbelief: "Be able to what?" She started to get irritable herself at this point - "Be held in captivity if the radiator wasn't switched on, especially in winter, it would be freezing"

As if he would have a choice...

I couldn't help the rant that followed: "Well, next time we're holidaying in the Middle East and four armed men stop our taxi and bundle us into the boot of a waiting car, blindfolded. I shall remember to ask them nicely if they wouldn't mind taking the chill off the room before we arrive, as my girlfriend is a bit nesh."

She didn't speak to me for the rest of the night. She went to bed, with a face that resembled a wet bank holiday in Cromer. Bloody Ross Kemp!! He should change the series title to Ross Kemp - extreme domestic violence.

So out of spite, I turned the heating off.

By the time I went to bed a few hours later, I was blue with cold!!! I didn't tell her, but she was right.

Brasilian's are shite

Isn't it strange the way the Americans and English speakers in a common tongue, but in so many ways, we don't know what each other is on about?

Ribald words, which to us are amusing, do not have the same impact, on the other side of 'The Pond'.

I am, of course, referring to the word fanny. In New York, it means bottom, lots of Americans have enormous 'fannies' even the blokes. You see, it's funny already – that's where it starts to get complicated, doesn't it?

A bloke with a fanny – good grief, surely not! I hear you say! Here in the UK, that's someone 'pre-op!' But in the good old USA, there are one hundred and fifty million blokes with 'fannies'. Everybody in America has a fanny. Half of them have knobs as well. What makes them men and women I hear you cry, I have no idea.

But in America, a "Fanny" is their bottom. Everyone has one! The point is the beauty of a language is that depending on where you are in the world, you can use a common word, but they mean completely different things.

In the UK and America, we both use the word shit, but if you say shite to an American, it doesn't mean anything. It doesn't exist in their vocabulary.

So, imagine the hilarious soccer commentary - from an American sports reporter - when I watched a soccer match in New York. I forget who was playing, but they always seem to have odd nicknames for their professional teams. It was something like the *Sacramento Willie Warmers*, playing the *San Jose Spanked Bottoms*.

Anyway, the thing I do remember was that a Brazilian player on the field was called Rafael Scheidt (Pronounced shite).

You would have thought that someone would have warned his mother before she married his father. I mean, if I had a girlfriend and she found out my name was Buster Haemorrhoid, she wouldn't be my girlfriend for long.

Rafael Scheidt (shite) was aptly named, because, he was!! He was the only Brazilian on the planet incapable of trapping a football or could pass it more than a few yards. Three-toed sloths in the jungle move more quickly over five yards than Mr. Shite.

As the game progressed, Rafael took a wild shot that went way over the crossbar. The commentator said: "And that was Scheidt". Indeed it was!!

Later in the game, a tricky winger ran down the touchline, and without so much as smirking, he said: "He tried to turn, but he ran into Scheidt"

The one that made me laugh the most was when he said of an opponent, "He had shite all over him".

A few years later, Rafael Scheidt turned up in Scotland. The weather matched his name I suppose. He played for Celtic for a while, but they had the good sense to put RAFAEL on the back of his shirt. However, everyone knew his surname, and opposing fans used to chant:

"You're Rafael and you know it"

Absolute Bliss!

Very occasionally, and I do mean only a few days per year, the conditions are right to perform the perfect stool. Of course, it comes as an absolute joy to the recipient, as, like a bloke passing his driving test on the first attempt, it is unexpected.

There are no omens, no premonitions, not a sign that it will happen. You don't look out the window - see eleven magpies, and think, oh eleven magpies, that must mean the perfect bowel movement. It just happens!!

Most of the year, a bowel movement is mundane, functional, slightly dull, rather time-consuming, and generally necessary. Unless of course, you have just won the lottery, in those circumstances, you could afford to have an endless supply of underwear, and never wear them more than once. But even then, you would soon lose friends, if every time you met them, you smelled like the 'great London stink of 1858'.

On very rare days, when, like the happy accident that spawned life on earth, all the conditions are right, and at that exact moment, everything is in perfect harmony, it can be a wondrous experience.

Having a perfect poo is the mark of a true craftsman, like Michel Roux with his *soufflé*, it has to be baked to perfection. Leave it too long and the moment will pass. It may even retreat - like an army on the run - back up your 'jacksie'.

The consistency has to be just right, to facilitate an effortless movement. Not too soft, not too hard, there must be no corners on it, and it has to be as smooth as a ball bearing.

To add to the scatological bliss, you must arrive in the bathroom at precisely the right moment. A slight urgency perhaps, but none of the button-popping desperate brow-sweating kerfuffle, associated with yanking your trousers down, as you are in danger of a 'boil wash'.

Once out in the open, the clean-up has to be effortless in the backside wiping department, and conservative use of toilet paper. Only then can you start to believe you may get a perfect ten.

They say the biggest telling-off is the one you give yourself. Let's be honest, self-analysis is a difficult thing. But to be content that you have done the utmost. To leave no disappointment, no doubts in the back of your mind, that you did your best, and have left no turd unturned, there is one last test you must pass, literally!!!

To gain the Olympic qualification, you must produce the magical David Nixon - 'disappearing jobbie'. Like a free diver holding his breath, disappearing into the abyss. You must produce a turd, that is under its own steam - that is a key criterion, under its own steam – no flush is required. The 'stealth' tommy slides silently unnoticed around the U- bend, leaving no trace, no 'pollards'. There must be no evidence you have ever been in the toilet.

The ghost poo is always a surprise. As you turn to take an affectionate look at all your good work, sadly you find...like a son on his eighteen birthday – the turd has left, gone without so much as a "cheerio". I always find myself - at that point - saying those immortal words from the cartoon Deputy Dawg, when Musky says: "Where did he go? Where did he go??" rubbing his eyes in disbelief.

The only indication you have been to the toilet - like toast in the kitchen, long after you've eaten it – is a familiar, yet unpleasant odour that lingers in the bathroom. The only blemish on a perfect scorecard is when someone shouts: "Christ – open the window!"

ABSOLUTE BLISS!!

This page is blank, as you may now need to go and have a comfort break.

Please use this page to write any amusing toilet stories, or mishaps of your own

Remember everyone has one good book in them!

Return to Sender

Sending a postcard should be an easy task. Let's face it, if mankind can put men on the moon, split the atom, and send photographs back from the outer reaches of our solar system - unless you were a pygmy in the Congo jungle or an IBAN tribal warrior in a remote part of Borneo - posting a letter to a loved one, from anywhere in the world, should be pretty straight forward.

Not so. Try posting something in Pakistan. Its proximity to India gives you a clue. Whatever you want to arrange, is going to be extremely long-winded, time-consuming, and utterly frustrating.

I only wanted to send one postcard to my parents, but it was like trying to organize a Rolling Stones concert in North Korea.

Taking a bus through the streets of Karachi, the bus was packed beyond capacity. People were sitting on the roof, on the bonnet, hanging off wing mirrors, and even sitting on the driver's knee. The bus was so overcrowded the driver was on another bus! After three minutes the oxygen had all but been used up, and I was forced to breathe in the rancid fumes of several camel-breathed locals, who probably hadn't cleaned their decaying teeth, or what remained of them since Pakistan broke away from India in 1948.

In addition, I was subjected to the endless and deafening sound of everyone on board - coughing up phlegm, and clearing their throats of various colourful stews of uncertain substances.

Hindi music was being forced through an inadequate music system at 400 decibels, temporarily deafening everyone onboard. The vibrations from which had made everyone onboard completely sterile.

I was sent to four different buildings in temperatures close to 40 degrees Celsius, each building at least half a mile apart, when finally, totally by accident, I stumbled across another building, which happened to be the right one. Soaked in sweat, and as tense as Andy Murray's tennis racket, I was dangerously close to having my first nervous breakdown. Upon arrival at the correct post office, I was informed, by a surly gentleman - with an arse like a Bombay money lender - after he cleared his throat and spat on the floor, just missing my big toe - that I was in block D, and the postmistress in charge of European mail was in block G.

Arriving in block G, I was pushed from an unnecessary lengthy queue to another lengthy queue, about five in all. By this time I was a familiar puce colour.

Finally, thank the Lord, I was in the right queue, but people started to push in, and from being third in line, I found myself at the back of a queue equal to any traffic jam on the M25 - on the August bank holiday.

I was finally served two and a half hours after the horrendous ordeal had begun, not at all certain the postcard would leave the building, let alone arrive at my parent's house, six thousand miles away.

Just for the record... I sent the postcard in 1986 and it never arrived, but due to the inefficiency of every part of daily life in Pakistan, I am still hopeful, it might!!

A funny Joke:

A very rich man has a servant called Walter, he calls down to Walter and says: "Walter run me my bath and be quick about it"

Water runs him a bath and the rich man starts his soak.

Suddenly Walter runs out of the room and comes back moments later with a water bottle.

The rich man stares in disbelief and says: "Walter what have you given me that for"

Walter replies: "Sir I thought you said, What about a water bottle Walter"

The rich man says: "All I did was fart!"

Shitting through the Eye of a Needle

The only good thing about getting cholera was that whilst I had it, I no longer had amoebic dysentery. And whilst not quite as life-threatening, it was draining, both physically and mentally. I couldn't trust myself, even the hint of a fart, had me in a right *'two-and-eight'*.and eight a bout of cholera was a godsend for both me and the restaurant lavatory. Because, until it was diagnosed, it had - like the swimming pool at New Brighton in the gales of 1989 - taken an absolute battering.

The fact I had cholera meant I had gone past the *sloople ploop* stage, as they say in Belgium. My body had given up alerting me to the fact I was about to shit myself. Indeed, it cut out the digestion process altogether. It went straight from plate to pan.

It had started with a form of irritable bowel that seemed to manifest every Thursday. It wasn't an irritable bowel - it was, quite rightly - AbsolutelFumingno idea what I ate on Wednesdays, but sure enough, every Thursday, I generally found myself, waiting for someone to finish in the only toilet in the building. Whilst waiting for patrons to vacate the bathroom, I had without realizing it, perfected, a very crude Nepalese version of *River Dance*.

Dreading every Thursday, I knew by end of breakfast service I'd be shitting through the eye of a needle. One day it was so bad, I decided to save time, and eat my breakfast on the toilet.

I occasionally had a little accident, and in an attempt to avoid taking my underpants off - or taking the rest of the day off, I tried wearing two pairs of underpants. 'skiddies' was an accurate description. Having said 'little accident' no accident is little if you 'follow through', all hands on deck, high priority stuff.

'Following through' - when you are serving customers, can be problematic. After all, everyone eats with all their senses: Sight, taste, and of course smell. There is nothing more off-putting, to spoil the dining experience, as a bloke is just about to order cottage pie, than catching a whiff of my freshly tainted trousers, smelling distinctly RIPE!!

I was just in the process of taking a family of four's breakfast order, but sadly, I never got as far as writing down scrambled eggs. I got as far as writing SCRAMBLE... then my pen went down. I did, however, scramble myself, pretty sheepishly to the toilet. I backed off apologizing as I retired. I never took another order. Writing the worSCRAMBLEMB was the last thing I ever did in that restaurant. An illustrious career cut short in its prime.

What I witnessed as I whipped off my trolleys - in that small dark room, will haunt me for the rest of my life. Staring back at me in my sodden 'smalls', dangling precariously just below my ' mushroom-in-a-bale-of-hay' was the undigested porridge I'd eaten only an hour earlier, it had been expelled, just as it had been swallowed, hot and steaming, albeit, having rested in my guts for an hour, it was now slightly overcooked.

I thought the end had come. It was time to meet my maker. I thought I was going to die. I went to seek medical help immediately. Quick thinking and an equally quick diagnosis saved my life.

Sadly, nothing saved my undergarments, not even two pairs had helped. Both had to be thrown away.

Later that day I looked out the window - a puppy had one pair on its head and was tossing the second pair into the air with its extremely sensitive nose. It didn't flinch at the nasal stinging stench rising from my badly soiled Y fronts, as it tore them to shreds.

Those undergarments had been with me ever since I'd left England. They had been at my side literally, every step of the way. We'd been through the good times and the bad. We had been through the 'loose' times as well as through constipation. Now they were confined to the great linen basket in the sky.

That puppy on the other 'paw' was as hard as nails!!

What a Dump!

Calcutta - Sunset over the Hugli River. Not exactly as inspiring as sunrise over Everest, but interesting to say the least.

They say Calcutta is a Black Hole, and it needs some TLC, but in a city of nine million, with a third of the population sleeping on the street, it is nothing short of fascinating.

The Howrath slums are on the southern side of the river, sitting, or should I say squatting, directly opposite Calcutta.

The problem with this part of the world is that even now, 27 years later, the vast majority of Indians have to poo *Al Fresco*. They do not have access to any toilet facilities at all.

That old nursery rhyme, S*kip, Skip, Skip To The Loo* was never more appropriate. On a boat trip down the Hugli, there were arses everywhere. Row upon row of the one-eyed sentinel lined the 'Tommy' strewn riverbank. There were more rusty Sheriff's badges on show than in a Clint Eastwood *Spaghetti Western.*

Men, women, and children squatted side by side on the banks of the river, creating rivers of poo. The stench in the air stung my enormous nostrils as I watched one wretched individual living in a sewer pipe, who appeared to have a prolapsed colon - 'drop one into the river. I talked, from a hundred feet away.

The problem was, and probably still is - the Hugli is quite fast-flowing. Great for those wiping their very exposed bums, but an absolute nightmare for those poor sods attempting to wash their faces thirty yards further down.

At one point I looked across at the banks at one bloke crapping five feet away from another bloke who was cleaning his teeth.

"Excuse me doctor – I have bad breath; can you suggest anything for halitosis?"

"Yes – clean your teeth upstream you fool!!"

Peel a grape

Unless you came from circus stock, not many people can claim to be shot out of a cannon.

Fewer people can claim to have done what I did whilst bathing myself in Christchurch, New Zealand.

I had been to the beach and was covered in sand, so decided to have a bath. The place I was staying had a huge, old, cast iron bath.

As I sat there contemplating life, I could feel a touch of wind brewing. As there was no one about, I thought I would force a fart, just to see how loud it could be. Old bath, high ceiling, lots of tiles, floor and walls, the optimum conditions for noise reverberation - perfect for a "bum trump".

I did peel one off. It was so loud I remember my daughter trumping once so loudly that it made her cry. Anyway, mine blew like a coronet player in a Cleo Laine jazz tribute. This was my own tribute - edition of 'The Last Post'!

As I farted, technically it is what we call in the trade - a 'dry shart' - something shot out of my bottom at quite a speed, and it hurt as it flew past my sphincter. Something made my eyes water!

Raising an alarmed eyebrow, I looked down and saw a small grape. It was baffling. I couldn't remember eating a grape, or anything with grapes in it, since I left England. I was dumbfounded.

On closer inspection, the grape still had a stalk attached. No wonder it hurt - a small piece of wood ripping down my rectum, embedding splinters in my colon.

Then it dawned on me, it wasn't a grape at all, well I suppose officially it was. What had shot out my arse was a swollen sultana.

Then I remembered. I'd had Muesli for breakfast!!!

John Holmes Eat your Heart Out

Long, long ago, before Man Utd kept winning silverware, there existed an era called the English First Division. To some, and in particular Sky Sports, it never happened. Like Pol Pot and the Cambodian killing fields - year zero: Before which all records were obliterated from the history books.

It was a time, so long ago, that most cars still had wind-down windows. Electric windows were only for posh people. And an ashtray in a car was an optional extra, and people boasted that their cars had headrests.

The year was 1992 and dinosaurs still roamed the earth. In those days it was perfectly acceptable to go out on a Saturday night, hit a girl over the head with a bit of four- by- two and take her back to your cave. " All above board your honour"!!

During this prehistoric period, my girlfriend invited her mother and brother for a six holiday to England. They came with the princely sum of thirty pounds between them.

I wasn't a skinflint, but I became reluctant to take any of my extended family to places, as it usually involved me spending large amounts of money. Especially when her brother started getting a taste for Guinness and Hagan Das ice cream.

I somehow ended up taking them to Knowsley Safari Park. I wish I hadn't bothered.

I have no idea what possessed her brother - who was sitting in the front passenger seat - to open the window. After all, it would be lunacy to go swimming if you could see a shark's fin in the water. Imagine - if a cobra started hissing at you, with its head bolt upright, no one would go over to it and flick it on the end of its nose.

This half-wit decided it might be a good idea to feed the elephants. Without asking, he wound down the window and started throwing grapes at the nearest one to the car. As all animals do, it sniffed the ground and picked up the grape with its trunk. We all thought it was a great idea - for about ten seconds. Next thing the elephant gets the idea there may be food in the car. And to everyone's abject horror, steps forward put its extremely long trunk through the open window and starts sniffing for food in the car. The nostrils were full of snot and dirt. To be honest I'd never seen an elephant trunk that closes before and could not believe how thick the hairs on its trunk were. They were like small chubby fingers.

In a blind panic the screams from everyone - but the half-wit, who was frozen in fear and howling like a werewolf - were some of the most disturbing sounds I have ever heard. Some of them were not even human.

As the screams intensified the elephant sniffing got a little more localized. Unfortunately for my passenger, the area earmarked for sniffing had moved to his groin.

The trunk suddenly swung from my now unsightly dashboard to his pitiful, mucus-stained crotch. No doubt the elephant could smell fear. I could! And if the half-wit hadn't soiled his pants, he must have dribbled uncontrollably from his ever-shrinking terrified meat, and what was now - 'no' veg. If I wasn't screaming myself, I might have felt sorry for him. Whilst he had brought all this danger upon himself, no one deserves to be manhandled by an elephant on the manhood. The enormous beast's sniffing proboscis dangled inches from the floor. I am of course referring to the elephant's trunk, not his sorry genitals.

By now the screams were so loud they were drowning out the radio. He was so scared he reverted to swearing in Polish. My girlfriend said he was screaming: "My wretched testicles". Indeed, he was in a very serious predicament.

I was only grateful it wasn't my 'John Thomas' being molested by this monstrous mammal. I did think about helping him by plucking a hair out of its nose, but I was frightened that might inflame the situation by annoying the beast. If I had done that, it may turn on me and trampled on my, as yet unpaid car. So, like the coward I was, I ignored his plea for help, and just screamed like a girlie!!

The shouting was so loud the baboons in the next field got agitated and started throwing their droppings at each other. To other cars, it must have seemed like the scene of mass murder.

Momentarily as the trunk extended from my brother-in-law's packet' I looked on with a mixture of resentment and envy at his new appendage: An eye-watering impressive phallus, with a mind of its own. I'm sure he could have gotten used to the 'John Holmes' look If it wasn't for the mucus-stained mess all over his trousers. I am not sure if the elephant had a cold, but the 'dew drops falling from its enormous 'conk', were ruining my car.

The poor bloke sitting beside me was frozen with fear. The screams had stopped, little more than an open mouth, and silence was coming out of his terrified and contorted face. He tried to scream but – nothing came out. He had his hands to his face and looked like *Monck's Scream.*

Time appeared to stand still, but the ordeal must have lasted less than a minute.

I turned to my girlfriend in the back seat and screamed for her to throw some fruit out the window. She threw the rest of the grapes and a few bananas out onto the grass verge. As quickly as it had begun, the elephant withdrew his offending trunk from the 'snot mobile' and started sniffing the fruit outside.

We wound the window up, as quickly as we could. We were mentally exhausted. We had been through a waking nightmare.

I know the signs in the park said: DO NOT EXCEED 10MPH, but I shot off so fast, I managed a skid mark on the tarmac.

When we got home, we both checked our underpants for skid marks of our own, independently of course, but gave each other a clean bill of health. Unlike my car, it needed a full valet costing £40.

I haven't been to the Safari Park since!

You can tell me I'm a Doctor

You are never at your best down below, when you are a bit off-colour, or you must expose yourself in public. A mixture of both is called a trip to the doctor.

To add insult to injury, my trip to the doctor involved showing him my 'John Thomas' in too much detail for my liking. I needed to be circumcised but had not got the bottle to go and make an appointment.

My boss at the time was a bit of a playboy, who had a string of women. He said I couldn't go through life, scared stiff to go 'tatties deep', just because my foreskin was too tight. He said he would sack me if I didn't make an appointment.

So, more alarmed that I might end up on the street, homeless and destitute, rather than lose the end of my 'John Thomas', I found myself in the doctor's surgery. I was too scared to tell him what the trouble was. I made up a tale that I had been having sore throats for months. He examined me and was convinced I had tonsillitis, and perhaps I should have them removed. Little did he know it wasn't my tonsils that needed surgery!

I did think it was a rather poor show that the doctor had looked down at my perfectly healthy throat and suggested that I needed my tonsils out. He even wrote me a prescription for some medicine to soothe my inflamed windpipe. Amazing! I know the NHS has cut back in recent years, but really, if that is the calibre of students we are recruiting into the profession, they should stay on the media studies course. To be honest, if he was that bad at medical diagnosis, there was no way he was going to be let loose anywhere near my 'Tackle' with a knife. I could ill afford any slip-up in that department. It isn't called a 'little man' for nothing!!

Almost convinced - I did have something wrong with my throat, I found myself thanking him, the fraudster and I turned to walk out. It was only when I got to the door, I plucked up the courage to say: "Well actually doctor...."

Next thing I know, he's saying: "Let's have a look at it then"

As I started to unbuckle my trousers, I could feel my manhood disappearing into my body. It resembled a sliver of mincemeat. My 'Laddo' was rather shy, to say the least. Nothing would coax it out from its hiding place, like a Moray eel hides in between the gaps in the coral reef. I felt awkward and ashamed. I should have been in the women's ward. It had disappeared, it was as if I'd jumped into a freezing mountain stream, then ran back into the surgery and immediately exposed my sorry-looking spring roll to the half-wit in the white coat.

 It looked like one of those embryonic baby kangaroos before they reach the safety of the pouch. Funnily enough, it did look a little like those things that hang down at the back of everyone's throat. Are they called uvula, and not a swollen one like he said I had? I ask you.

The doctor put on a monocle. I kept thinking it was a miniature magnifying glass.

He then put my minuscule manhood on the end of his pencil. He raised an eyebrow and kept saying: "Hmm – dear me".

 Good job it wasn't a 6-inch rule. Okay, you horrid little man – I thought – "Don't rub it in. Don't make it any more embarrassing than it already is – You could be kind and boost my confidence – Say something nice like - Wow!" I felt like saying: "Get yours out then and see how smug you are". But I thought it might sound a little bit homoerotic.

Instead, I was apologetic, and openly made a joke about the size, saying: "I bet you don't get many mules in here". At that point, he furrowed his brow so tightly that his monocle fell out onto the floor.

Inside I was shouting: "For god's sake grow". I even tried to think of rude thoughts to make it grow, but all I could think of was burning tyres and Margaret Thatcher!!!

Hovis: Great bread, terrible bog paper

In the days of General Tito's tenure at the helm, he impressively held together six, possibly seven (if you include Kosovo) nations with little more than an iron fist and a loud, angry voice, and he called it Yugoslavia. In the recent past after all the fall-out in the Balkans, some people look back on his reign with rosy coloured spectacles.

I look back on my time in Yugoslavia with less than rosy coloured testicles, but with fond nostalgia.

An inquisitive teenager, from the windswept Northwest of England, whose only previous chance, of seeing anyone with their top off at the beach, was seeing their uncle in a string vest, walking his dog along Prestatyn promenade on a partially warm day. So suddenly to discover that raven-headed beauties were prancing around in little more than Chanel No. 5 on sunny beaches 'abroad', was quite a thrill.

Indeed, Yugoslavia was 'abroad', and compared to everywhere I had been, it was hot and exotic.

All the blokes were tanned and heavily moustached, with dark greased-back hair. It was the sort of place Brad Pitt would feel inadequate. He'd feel as handsome in Yugoslavia as Lyle Lovett. After holidaying in Yugoslavia 'The Pitts' would take to plastic surgery. Forget going home and unpacking – They would ask their driver to take them - straight to a cosmetic surgeon.

They may have been handsome, but unlike 'The Pitts, Yugoslavs were not blessed with wads of cash, their wallets were as bare as *Old* Mother *Hubbard's Cupboard,* and consequently, for them to feed their growing families, due to the fact, every northern European lady who set eyes on them, was pregnant half an hour after meeting them. They were all forced to work on the black market, to make ends meet. Everyone did 'things' on the side, to make extra dinars.

We had heard there was a nudist beach just around the headland, and if the beach we were on, was anything to go by, there would be busloads of Eastern Europeans parading in the buff, frolicking like Yorkshire Terriers on heat. The two of us were rather keen to find out if this *Shangri la* existed.

The problem was, I didn't mind looking, but I didn't particularly want anyone to look at me, I certainly didn't want to 'drop my trolleys', and show the Yugoslavs, what put the 'Great' in Britain, because to be honest, it wasn't great at all.

The beach we wanted to go to could only be accessed via an extremely long walk, or by boat and beyond the headland.

Once there, it would be obvious we were not nudists. We were both worm-white and blistered on a sunny day in December. It was obvious that our bodies hadn't been exposed in any way, shape, or form, since birth.

So, we hired a canoe from a dashingly handsome, unkempt chap, with the most outrageous handlebar moustache and equally outrageous - fake leather - bright red, crocodile skin boots - and a jumper that had seen better days. He must have worn it, every day of Tito's reign, and hadn't washed it since. It was threadbare and looked like a dog had got hold of the sleeve and started to run down the beach with it in his mouth.

We crossed his grubby palm with silver and paddled out to sea.

The tide and current were quite strong, and the headland was a little further than we had anticipated.

In no time at all, the great effort, the sun, and the Yugoslavian goulash we had eaten at lunchtime, all started to take their toll.

A mile from the headland, and at least half a mile from the beach we had just left - in the middle of the Adriatic - I wanted a poo. I was in deep water, both metaphorically and literally. I did think about 'launching' it over the side, but unless I had the poise and balance of Nadia Comaneci on the narrow beam, there was absolutely no way I could do my 'business' - without the canoe capsizing. I didn't fancy having to try and get back into the canoe in such deep water. I didn't have the strength.

The only thing to do was head for the rocky islet about a hundred yards away. I wasn't sure what I would do when I got there, but at least it was " terrafirma". It may even offer a little bit of privacy, me the ocean, my mate, and a canoe.

By the time we got there, I was ready to explode - like a suicide bomber.

I gingerly got out of the canoe and onto the rocky outcrop, and with much relief dropped my shorts.

My mate said he had no idea what I was going to clean myself up with. Neither had I. That scenario – wiping your bottom after going to the toilet! What an odd concept.

He only had a daypack, and we had little more than a few sandwiches. Regrettably, and a little foolhardy, I said: "That will have to do".

Next thing I know, as I'm swiping a cheese and pickle 'sarnie' across my arse pickle, it fell apart into a million crumbs up my back passage.

My ring-piece looked like Andromeda, some far-flung galaxy.

To add to my plight, a seagull swooped down and pinched one of the sandwiches!!

In the end, I was in a sorry state. Christ, it was a mess, what a fiasco. It was as though someone had said to a three-year-old: "Paint a picture of a house on that man's bottom"

I was stuck on a rock in the sea, arms out, covered in my squalor, squatting like a cormorant drying its wings.

My 'Dag' had gotten everywhere, even on my shoe. It was utter humiliation. It had been the worst idea since Kennedy said to his driver: "Turn left past that grassy knoll".

I had no pride left. I was spent. I had to rid myself of these apocalyptic 'dingleberries'.

I closed my eyes, looked to heaven, and fell backward into the sea, like an abalone fisherman. Arse and tackle in full view, as though watching some sort of weird pornographic baptism.

We never did see any nudists, but my mate did see my nether region - smeared in its own 'doings' - do a perfect swallow dive into the crystal-clear waters of the Adriatic. In a matter of moments, the water quality dropped, and the nearest beach lost its blue flag rating!!

Just shows you how fickle Europe is and after that Brexit was inevitable.

Noisy Neighbours

Many years ago, I opened a magazine and saw an advert that said: *Nepal – the roof of the world, most people will only see it in an atlas.*

From that moment on, I knew I was destined to travel.

I lived in Kathmandu for four months, on the top floor of a block of flats, which I shared with an extremely eccentric American called Mr. McKinney. He talked in riddles and only stopped for breath when he was in danger of passing out. He had a very high opinion of himself, was good at everything, and what was left in the world to be achieved, he alone was attempting.

He delighted in telling anyone that would listen, whether animal, vegetable, or mineral, that he lived in Cambridge Massachusetts, and lived ten minutes' walk from Harvard. He also delighted in telling people that since he moved there twenty years earlier, his IQ had increased by 35 percent.

He was born in the wrong country. He should have been born in Nepal, for he was a devout Buddhist, and wore Nepalese clothing underneath his Harris Tweed jacket, with a badge of King Birendra on his lapel. He wore the traditional striped Nepalese prayer cap, and he never went anywhere without it. In the four months, he lived next door, I couldn't tell you if he had more hair than a Rastafarian, or if he was as hairless as a boiled egg.

He had a bright red nose, which had a blackhead on the end of it the size of a marrowfat pea. Every time I saw him, I wanted to squeeze him. But I feared if I extracted the offending blackhead, his face might cave in. Indeed, if it shot out of his nose, the pressure built up behind it may sever my head.

He referred to the King of Nepal as His Majesty. He delighted in spouting off about how many times he had been in the Himalayas – four times in one year.

The reason for such frequent visits to Nepal was due to his having some very influential friends, who were all minted, as was he, or so he said. They had formed a business consortium to legally cultivate cannabis, as a drug for cancer patients. In most parts of the world, commercial cannabis cultivation was illegal, but not in Nepal at the time.

By day I could hear the tapping of his typewriter, and by night I had the misfortune, along with everyone else on the sixth floor, to be subjected to Mr. McKinney's one love. That love was music. Unfortunately, music didn't feel the same way about him. God had not given him the gift of song. In short, his rendition of Cat Stevens' ballad *Morning Has Broken* sounded as if Mr. McKinney's voice just had.

One night, Mr. McKinney's frequent trips to Nepal were cut short, and he was never to return. It was a very quick decision on his part. It started with an altercation. Some locals living nearby were fed up with the noise in the middle of the night and went around to the flat to confront him.

They cornered him on the stairs. To be fair they did wait until he had finished his very bad rendition of *Knocking On Heaven's Door,* and promptly knocked on his. They dragged him out, protesting and screaming like girlies. They forced his head through the banisters, twice, and generally gave him a good, old-fashioned - public school – Beating, trousers down style.

His calls for assistance to his one and only friend in Nepal, Doctor Singh - a fat bearded Indian who told terrible lies, not least that he was a doctor, a pal of Ranjiv Gandhi, and had graduated from Sandhurst - went predictably unanswered. Doctor Singh did make a brief appearance on the landing, to see what all the fuss was about.

He made full use of his military training - adopting stealth tactics, by slipping cowardly and unnoticed into the nearest toilet, locking himself in until the altercation passed. I, like the doctor, had no intention of helping the man, and watched from the safety of the floor above, as Mr. McKinney's head went careering through the banister rails for a third and final time, this time minus his hat.

In the morning, after a brief detour to the police station to file a complaint against the locals, he went to the airport and flew home to increase his IQ further, and to start martial arts for beginner classes.

Incidentally - he was bald as a coot!!

Secret Agent 002 Bond – Basildon Bond!!

I've often wondered what it would be like to be Daniel Craig, well not the real Daniel Craig, his character James Bond.

It looks like such a glamorous lifestyle being a spy, so adventurous.

Skiing in the Alps in the morning, being chased through the Dolomites by an assassin, base jumping to safety, driving a brand-new *Aston Martin* to a secret rendezvous with a gorgeous Russian agent, and then lunch in Venice. Then in the afternoon, pick up your very own *Sunseeker* power boat, whisk Agent Petrova off to a secluded island, to spend the night dipping your parsnips in the cheese *fondu*, before being flown home in the Prime Minister's very own *Learjet*, to be knighted by the queen by the following lunchtime.

This plot could apply to any of the 'Bond' movies. Fleming must have been one of the laziest writers in history - Sitting on his shaded terrace - in Jamaica, sunbathing, drinking blue mountain coffee by the bucket full, Bob Marley blaring out on his ghetto blaster all day. Laziness is only matched by the designers of a famous Stuttgart car manufacturer - every car since 1950 looks the same!

If you want real adventure, I'm your man. Try getting from Bombay to London with twenty quid in your pocket.

I was sitting in the departure lounge at Bombay Airport, waiting for the check-in desk to open, when a Dutch man came and sat by me. We got talking, and he asked me where I was headed. I told him I was flying to Athens. I intended to fly back to Greece and start picking fruit so that I could earn enough money to get back to *'Blighty'*.

I'd spent the night in the airport, along with hordes of locals. I'm not saying I didn't trust them, but, during that particular night, I learned the art of sleeping with one eye open.

It was only when I asked him if he was going to Athens, that I realized the flight landed in Athens, but it then carried on to Amsterdam. That was where the man was headed.

The cogs started to turn, slowly at first. I realized the plane would land, some people would get off, others would get on, and the rest of the passengers would stay in their seats for half an hour, before taking off again.

Amsterdam is a lot closer to England than Athens, and more importantly, the chance of earning more money, and possibly factory work, was greater in Holland.

Just one moment I thought. My ticket said Athens, and that is where my bags would be heading.

Then again, what bags? I had a rucksack with a few old clothes and a sleeping bag in it. That was it!!

If I left my sleeping bag in the departure lounge and took my rucksack on the plane as hand luggage, my rucksack would be always with me.

As the check-in opened and I stepped forward, I started to sweat like a Racehorse in a sauna.

The woman behind the desk asked me where I was headed, and I heard myself say: "Athens".

I felt like I was a drug smuggler, but she put her head down and carried on processing my tickets. She asked me for bags, and I heard myself say: "No – just hand luggage". She looked at my rucksack for what seemed like a minute, but was only a second, then handed me back my passport with my boarding card.

Once I was armed with my boarding card, I was home free. At the departure gate, the stewardess asked for my passport and boarding pass. Once on board, I noted the aircraft was half empty, so I sat in my seat until we took off, then I moved to a different seat. The plane was less than half empty because anyone with half a brain would fly KLM to Amsterdam.

As we landed in Athens for a brief stop, my heart almost did. I was as nervous as a kitten. I thought the stewardess would come over to me and say: "Hey aren't you supposed to be getting out here?" but she didn't. She just walked up the aisle and smiled. She asked if I would like to move to a less cramped section of the plane. What a result – no one could touch me now. I was now officially in a different seat to my boarding pass, and if anyone questioned me, I could blame the 'trolley dolly'.

Taking off for Amsterdam, I knew I couldn't be thrown off the plane. It did cross my mind – The joke about the overloaded aircraft. The pilot says to the passengers they will have to lighten the load somehow.

So - the American shouts – "Remember the Alamo", then throws the Mexican out of the plane. I gave a wry smile. It couldn't happen

- Could it? Not to me. A burly Mancunian hurls the Scouser out the window. Job done!

As we landed in Schiphol, I felt slightly guilty. Of course, once in Holland, no one asks to see your boarding pass, immigration was only interested in my passport. The immigration official was also interested in a pair of foul-smelling socks in my rucksack, which I'd forgotten to throw out at Bombay airport.

The sniffer dog made a yelping noise as she found the offending item. However, no one in the building was bothered by how I'd arrived in Holland, they were not interested. I'd got a passport, and that was good enough.

Walking out of the airport terminal, minus a pair of stinking old socks, I did feel like James Bond and relieved. I had thought the unpleasant 'whiff', - detected in the air around seat 35E - was my overactive sweat- gland.

It was then I started to think, perhaps I could get to England.

My next obstacle was the train from Amsterdam to Oostende. I still had my twenty pounds, but I may need that for the Channel crossing. My best bet was to board the train and do my best to avoid the ticket collector. I did extremely well until we got close to the Belgium border. In those days they still had passport control. Border control usually arrived at the same time as the ticket collector, and that was going to be tricky.

It was then I noticed a carriage of teenage schoolchildren. I opened the door to their carriage, and thankfully most Dutch youngsters speak very good English. I explained the situation and asked if I could I hide under the seat. They loved the idea and agreed to hide me. I was a stowaway. This was the stuff of James Bond. They let me crawl under the seat, sat down, and placed bags in the gaps between their feet, blocking me from view.

They were giggling with enthusiasm, but I was very frightened indeed.

I could end up in jail. I heard a man's voice say: "Tickets", then another man says: "Passports". Moments later they were gone. I'd done it.

Before long I found myself at the ferry terminal. I had twenty pounds and an interrail card that was a year out of date, it might just work I thought.

The cost of a single, four-hour crossing to Dover was twenty-two pounds. I told the cashier I had an interrail card which entitled me to half-price ferry crossings. I just flashed him the brown wallet, and thankfully, he nodded and asked for eleven pounds.

I'd done it, Victorious, I had travelled from Bombay to England in less than a day, and still with nine pounds to spare.

As we set sail, I sat back in the chair, exhausted. I wasn't exhausted enough not to notice a fine pair of breasts belonging to a statuesque French lady sitting opposite. Her shapely form puts an unnatural strain on her blouse buttons. I closed my eyes, and smiled, as thoughts of those cool Himalayan nights came flooding back!!

Grandad's trowel

My grandad had two vices, well only two that he would own up to. One was smoking and the other was drinking.

In those days everyone smoked, but eighty to a hundred fags a day could be described as an addiction rather than a vice. As for the drinking, it was only in the latter years that he drank at home, and by drink, I am referring to the three-fingered whisky. An extremely generous measure- he only gave to himself and his family.

He used to get very upset by alcohol frugality, almost angry. He once made a major purchase, and when everything had been completed, the vendor offered my grandad a whisky to celebrate. He said that the measure the bloke gave him was so small that it hardly covered the bottom of the glass, and by the time he had lifted it to his lips, the whisky had evaporated.

He would have three whiskies on the trot and then go to bed. Nine fingers of whisky every day could also be described as an addiction.

When he was in his prime, we are talking between the age of twenty-five and forty-five, he spent a good percentage of those twenty years in the pub

It caused many an argument. As my nanna used to complain that in all their married life, he never took her out for a meal. His response to this was pragmatic - why should he waste money eating in restaurants when there was food at home? My nanna replied that it was a pity he didn't apply that logic to the money he blew in the pub with his many friends.

The owner of the pub - 'Bear and Staff' in Gateacre, had put three children through private school from the money my grandad put through his till.

He never actually gave up drinking, but he did pack in the smoking. He gave up in 1976 when cigarettes went up to fifty pence a packet. The precise moment was during the 1976 Wimbledon final. *Borg* was playing *Nastase*. It was a swift decision on his part. He was puffing smoke like a Liverpool slum in 1878 and had lit up so frequently that the smoke billowing from the open kitchen window had alerted a farmer who thought the house was on fire and called the fire brigade. The roasting he got off the enraged fire officer and the subsequent one from my nanna was so severe that his trousers were in danger of spontaneously combusting.

The result was – he spent a week in the doghouse, which was quite handy, as the dog had recently died and the kennel was empty. After his week in solitary confinement, he gave up smoking!

However, my nanna said there was something far more sinister than cigarettes and alcohol. My grandad couldn't resist buying tools. My nanna would walk him the long way around a shopping centre on pension day, to avoid the DIY shop next to the supermarket, or there would be no money left for food.

His garage and shed were so full of tools that there was little room to squeeze himself in the garage, never mind the car. It looked like a 'Screwfix warehouse. Many of them were unopened and unused, and there were several that even my grandad hadn't

a clue what they were used for. My nanna quite rightly asked him if he didn't know what they were used for, and why he wasted money on them. He never had a good answer.

His tool 'vice' was collecting trowels, and like a heroin addict stealing for his next fix, he would go thirty miles out of his way, just to buy a trowel. The local hardware store in Mold had dedicated half his store to trowels, just because he knew my grandad would part with cash. He had even turfed out a double-glazing salesman who was renting a corner of his shop. The business was brisk all times of the year, as my grandad frittered away his pension, on the next trowel.

It was a 'no brainer for the local shopkeeper – buy the trowels and he will come. Like a fisherman chumming the water for a Great White. Mr. Griffiths became North Wales shopkeeper of the year on the back of my grandad's addiction.

During the summer holidays, my mum and dad used to take me to my grandads and leave me there for the week. I loved it, and so did he. However, on one such visit, I had a touch of "obstruction" as they refer to constipation in Poland, it all built up, so that by the Thursday, when I eventually went, I produced a stool so big it stood proud of the water by a good six inches, and like the iceberg that sunk the titanic, the main body of my Elvis killer was hidden below the surface.

 That was the problem – sinking it. There was no way the oversized feculence would go down without a fight. Forcing it to flush was difficult, like a removals man trying to get a king-size bed up a flight of stairs and around a tight-cornered landing single-handed.

To be honest, I was only a child, and at the time, unaware of my grandad's flushing frenzy, to remove the unwanted intruder from his property.

He tried everything, talking nicely to the idle turd, shouting at it, good cop bad cop. He tried writing an official letter to the council. His water bill soared as he hopelessly flushed to try and evict the hapless 'Tommy'. Nothing would shift this illegal squatter.

After a good half hour, my poor old granddad was, like my bowel, absolutely spent. The last time he had such a vigorous workout was when he'd been for his annual medical. He sat down, opened the bottle of 'Bell's,' and pondered his predicament.

It was whilst he was sipping happily on the tumbler full, that he remembered the tools in his overcrowded garage.

He went out into the garden and reappeared forthright and reinvigorated. He was a man on a mission.

Like a madman with a claymore during the *Battle of Culloden,* in an act that can only be described as sacrificial, my grandad held aloft a brand new trowel, and with the eye of the precision engineer that he was, chopped my 'deposit', my Viking longboat, into something resembling one of those large Toblerone bars you get at Xmas.

As he did so, an almost demonic smile came across his face, as he turned to my nanna and said: "You see Joyce, I told you that trowel would come in handy".

When my dad came to pick me up the following weekend, my grandad took him to one side and said without a hint of irony, that I had laid the biggest 'turkey' he had ever seen.

He added that it must have stretched the lad's sphincter like a rattlesnake eating a squirrel.

He suggested with some concern that my dad should take me to the doctor to get checked out. It may lead to problems later on in life if he ignored it.

Sadly my dad ignored his advice and I can report – forty-seven years after the squalid incident happened, I am still having toilet issues. Indeed, only last week I produced another Elvis killer so enormous, it not only made my eyes water but my daughters too.

It was big enough to work. It was issued with a national insurance number immediately upon its temporary arrival into this world. However, due to advances in plumbing over the years, it slipped around the U bend without a problem.

My own "U bend" was stinging for days.

Even last night I had to resort to medicated toilet paper with a soothing Aloe Vera triple ply.

Fluff's bottom

Spending forty-five pounds on a good night out is a pleasurable experience, even better if you don't remember getting home. However, spending forty-five pounds in the launderette, because someone else's cat has crapped on your duvet eight days on the trot, is infuriating, to say the least.

There is nothing better, after a hard day at the office than getting home and finding a cat turd in the middle of your bed.

"Hello, Darling, and what has your day been like?" "Oh, very busy – lots of meetings and paperwork!" "Hello, Fluff and how has your day been?" "Fantastic, I slept all day, then I woke up, and ate a few of those prawns you left me, suddenly I realized that I needed the toilet but couldn't be 'arsed' having a dump in the cat litter, so I just did it on your blanket, thanks for asking – Tell you what it was so much fun, I'll do it again tomorrow" - Marvellous!

I have to say that Fluff may only be a small cat, but the stools she produces are a big problem.

It all started when I moved in with my then girlfriend, now wife, and Fluff didn't like the fact that I was now the cat's pyjamas, not her. I had moved in on her "patch" and so, started to mark her territory, with stool aplenty.

They are so pungent that one night it did a feline 'Tommy' in the cat litter and the smell woke me up with a slap in the face, the stench was that bad

I'm sure if you asked a Kurdish village in Northern Iraq, whom they would prefer, an onslaught from Saddam's army or for Fluff to walk into town, they would opt for 'Chemical Ali' every time. That makes Fluff a very dangerous cat indeed.

So, imagine how I felt when I was told that Fluff had a bout of 'loose stool' and the shite had got stuck to its fur, and would I be an angel and wash its bottom.

Of course, my girlfriend, who owned the cat, was barking instructions from the safety of the lounge, she was insisting I snipped the fur around its rusty sheriff's badge.

Snip around the ring piece of a distressed cat indeed, you try it.

To be honest, I don't even snip the fur around my arse, never mind something with sharp claws and bites an extremely supple gymnastic from the old Eastern Bloke, with a very long pair of scissors and a dentist mirror would have trouble trimming their rear nether region. But they would have better luck than mc, I grant you that.

Fluff was twisting like a saltwater crocodile in a death roll – As I was gingerly trying to snip around its anus with the precision of a sailor performing brain surgeon on the difficult leg around Cape Horn. The cat was enraged, as I would be. It was impossible.

To make matters worse, my girlfriend could hear its distressing cat calls for help, and was yelling – "Don't hurt it, don't hurt it"

"Don't hurt it – If it tries to bite me one more time, I'll wring its neck".

Next thing I lose my grip and it shoots across the draining board, its tail wagging like a dog that's got a dinosaur bone for Xmas, showering me in droplets of cat muck. Cups and saucers were flying everywhere. I tried to stop the cat's feculence from spoiling the crockery and bravely took one to the head, just above my left eyebrow.

In the meantime, she is still on the phone in the lounge and periodically yelling: "What have you broken? – try not to make a mess". I think they call it multitasking, and blokes are not very good at it. However, back to the cat fiasco -Too late to say don't make a mess, I'm in a sorry state. Far worse than the cat at this point.

The smell was atrocious, and not from the cat, from my eyebrow, I started to balk. The not completely firm stool was starting to drip from my eyebrow onto my nose, like melting snow on the tundra after the Springtime thaw.

It was like a scene from the Exorcist, and I was Linda Blair. As I went in close to mow around its overactive anus, one last time, the frightened feline played her trump card and shat on my scissors.

I'd had enough. I filled the sink with warm water and sank its wretched, filthy backside into the water. The cat, as I did, looked very bedraggled indeed. I looked like something the cat had dragged in, and the cat looked like it had dragged itself in.

Slightly off guard, I let my grip on its neck loosen, and with that, in an act of stoic defiance, it swung around and sank its teeth into my finger.

I never finished cleaning up its 'Tommy' strewn backside, or the sink unit for that matter.

Instead, I spent the next three hours in Accident and Emergency at Fazakerly Hospital, as a cat bite can kill you. Well, that's what it said on the pamphlet in the waiting room.

And all I wanted to do was kill that cat!

Turd in a phone box

Blondie once wrote a very famous hit called *"Hanging on the telephone"* and it got to number one.

I, on the other hand, had something - "Hanging on the telephone" and it was number two.

When I say it was hanging, I mean smeared – right around the earpiece. I'm shaking my head just thinking about it.

Some 'little shit' had decided it might be fun to cover the telephone receiver with a 'big shit' – a sizeable piece of dog dirt, He had managed to make his creation of a turd sculpture, which resembled a half-eaten walnut whip.

These were the days when mobile phones were only seen in episodes of *Star Trek*. Therefore, if you happened to be out and about, and you wanted to call someone, you had to use a public phone box.

On this particular occasion, I wanted to speak to a girlfriend I had met at Pontins whilst on holiday, and I didn't want my mum and dad listening in to my conversation, so I walked down the street to the nearest public phone.

In those days I had a luxuriant head of hair, long and flowing, not unlike a Shetland Pony, galloping across a field in a high wind.

Anyway, I was on the phone with this girl in Birmingham, when I got a distinct impression, I had stood in dog muck.

The smell in the close confines of the phone box was purulent, I tried not to balk. At first, I thought it was on my shoes, I kept lifting my shoe, first the left one, then the right one, like a strange impression of Larry Grayson. But the soles of my shoes were clean as a whistle. I thought, what the hell is that smell, and where in all that is holy is it coming from? My eyes were watering like I was slicing an onion.

The smell made me addled and confused. I was punched drunk.

No matter how hard I searched I could not locate the source of the emanation. Then I realized every time I turned my head to the receiver the stench was unbearable. I looked at my 'snorkel'. Not the 'snorkel' we take to the beach.

A snorkel before 1980 was a type of 'parka' jacket with a long zip hood that made everyone wearing one, look like - Uncle Bulgaria from the Wombles.

It was only when I went to scratch my head that I realized there was dog dirt behind my fingernail. Thirty seconds earlier my nails were as neat as beauticians, and moments later, filthy as a child chimney sweep in 1890.

At the same time as I smelt the ungodly stench, I did notice a distinct dampness around my ear but thought it was my wet hair. It was then I discovered the gruesome truth. My hair was caked in dog shite. It was all over the left side of my head. My ear was brown with 'doggie doo'. I looked like a *black and white minstrel* drawn by *Picasso*.

I turned to look at the telephone receiver to discover a single canine 'chocolate brownie' complete with the lollypop stick poking out of it.

I terminated the call immediately, dropped the phone, and I ran home, and had a bath, for the second time in less than an hour. I was incandescent with rage. I'd just put another 50p in the pay phone.

As I ran home, I was grateful that the sky was turning dark. I encountered the humiliation of meeting one very attractive girl from my class enroute to home. If it had been daylight, she would have seen the 'organic' hearing aid I had just acquired, but unless she had been fathered by an owl, she wouldn't be able to see my faecal earmuff in the dimming light. She may not be able to see it, but boy, could she smell it!

The steam was rising from my 'Davy Crockett's hat' like a lake of hot bubbling mud. Remarkably, she seemed to ignore the stench emanating from my person, and I noticed she surreptitiously lifted the sole of her shoe and looked down at it. She assumed she had stepped in something. I could tell she was in a hurry to halt the conversation. How embarrassing, meeting the girl of your dreams and not only being tongue-tied but smelling like a Victorian Sewer and looking like an H-block dirty protester all at the same time.

As she set off for home, she paused under a streetlamp to take a closer look at the phantom turd on the bottom of her shoe.

I too was keen to get home myself to rid myself of the cow pat *tamoshanter* that I was temporarily wearing.

To make matters worse my long-distance relationship ended abruptly that night, as she complained I'd rudely put the phone down on her. She was deeply offended.

Rudely put the phone down indeed – what about me - someone had 'rudely' covered the handset I was using, in Cavalier King Charles Spaniel 'dingleberry', the remains of which were now plastered against the side of my head. I looked like something out of an episode of *Doctor Who.*

However, every turd has a silver lining - I was quite relieved she finished with me to be honest, as she lived in Birmingham, and I couldn't drive at the time.

FOOTNOTE – I found out only recently my second cousin had a habit in his youth of smearing telephone box receivers in animal "doings". He said that the phone box on the corner of Longview was his favourite.

At least he kept it in the family!!

"A Hazelnut in every bite"

I find it strange when people say that their dog is very intelligent, or that their budgie is very clever because let us face it, animals are not clever at all. Can they do mathematics? – No, not even the most basic calculations. Can any animal take the top off a bottle of Calpol? – No, they can't. Can they make a pyramid out of playing cards – Not very likely.

On graduation day at Sheffield University has anyone cheered for the Guinea pig in the cap and gown – No, and they never will. Animals are as likely to finish the Times crossword, as Mansfield Town winning the Premiership.

Watch out Oppenheimer there is a squirrel in our garden, with a theory on nuclear fusion, which will put doubt in the minds of the scientific fraternity and expose you as a fraud.

As for Einstein's theory of relativity, it's not a patch on Brian the snail's thesis on thermodynamics. You get my drift!!

Animals generally live outside and live by instinct. Insects and small rodents live in gardens, and they hunt under the cover of darkness and tend to garden hop within their territory, which they mark with their urine – very clever indeed!

Humans, well one did exactly that, but under the cover of darkness and the influence of alcohol.

My mate Miguel, you met him in the other book. Well Miguel, liked to mark his territory, especially, when he had had a 'skin full'. He had a 'skin full' most days. Basie wis hat we in the medical trade refer to as a 'piss head'.

We had been to the pub, to celebrate Boxing Day. As usual, Miguel was drinking excessively and started to make a nuisance of himself. The landlord was getting fed up with his rowdy behaviour and had him thrown out when he placed his testicles on the pool table baize and shouted to the bloke who was just about to pot – "How about this for a difficult pink!"

As the 'bouncer' bounced him out of the pub, whilst Miguel was swiftly trying to place his tackle, which at that point was bouncing uncontrollably, back in his trousers, we followed in hot pursuit.

When we got outside - Miguel was missing. He seemed to have disappeared, slipping not so silently, into the wintery night. I wasn't particularly concerned that he was missing. He had made a career of avoiding a 'good hiding' after upsetting someone, whilst he was in a drunken stupor.

One time he upset a bloke in a public phone box when he dropped his trousers and rubbed his bare bottom on the phone box glass. The bloke was furious, he was ready to give Miguel a beating – I stepped in and had to calm the man down. Miguel just laughed and ran off. Well, he pulled his pants up first.

So, getting back to the story. I knew he would turn up at some stage, we were staying at my parent's house, and he had the address.

At half past four in the morning, everyone was sound asleep. They were awoken by Miguel ringing the doorbell. Unfortunately, my dad was first downstairs. He opened the door to this 'creature' an alien life form. Miguel was partially clothed, covered in soil, and had twigs and turf in his hair. He looked like Corporal Jones from *Dad's Army* on a night practice of the Normandy Landings.

My dad did not bother to say anything to him. He turned around and went back to bed, leaving Miguel to shut the front door. A task - even my pet dog Skippy had managed at one point. Sadly - Miguel was unable to match the canine at such a difficult task and left the front door wide open until morning, in the middle of Liverpool!

A task he did manage, however, which needed the cunning of a safecracker, was to pick the lock of my dad's drinks cabinet and help himself to a bottle of my father's pride and joy – a bottle of *'Wild Turkey' Bourbon.*

The next morning my dad's outrage at seeing the front door open was magnified tenfold when he discovered the half-empty contents of his beloved bottle of 'Wild Turkey'. The steam rising from his ears was slightly less alarming than the colour his face was turning. I don't think Dulux could match that shade of red. He looked like an aubergine with ears.

I was rather upset that my dad was giving me a right good telling off, I hadn't done anything wrong. My mum came in with a face like thunder and piled on the pressure with a rant equally upsetting and a little more embarrassing.

She told me she had just been in the spare room when Miguel was taking a shower. Probably - a cold one. She was most upset and could not get her words out. She is very religious and does not like anything rude, risqué or slightly ribald. My mum once went into the butcher's and seeing a young lad behind the counter could not bring herself to say Breast of chicken, so asked for a chicken chest and blushed. She calls Blue Tits – Blue ones!

 She finally got her words out and said - and I quote "I'm not having a grown man soiling himself like that in my own home". I asked her to explain, it was as if I'd soiled myself, and she was livid.

She said "he" raising her eyes upstairs - not mentioning his name "has not managed to get to the toilet in time, and now I'll have to change the bed". I said, "Has he wet the bed?" she sternly replied "I don't know about that – but I can see he has dirtied it, and himself" – She looked at me, and I felt like a naughty schoolboy. I may as well have been Ronnie Biggs.

 I lowered my head in shame. I indeed was a grown man, and I was taking the 'can' for someone else's intolerant bowel. I wanted to say, "But what has that got to do with me – I didn't tell him to do it" But I just stood there taking my punishment. I was waiting for the black cloth to be put on my mum's head and for her to say, "Take him down from this place, and may god have mercy on your soul".

My parent's left the room, and I tried to enjoy my breakfast – Alone. It was rather difficult, for two reasons, I couldn't get the unsightly stain out of my mind, even though I hadn't seen it, and as it was *coco pops* the milk had turned brown. I suddenly didn't feel all that hungry.

When Miguel came downstairs, he looked so sheepish, a farmer would have mistaken him for *Dorset Down*. Before I could say anything to him, he asked for a wet cloth. I said, "Wet cloth! my mum needs to buy a new bed". He said, "I don't know what you mean". I told him what my mum had told me and, in a voice that can only be described as abject relief - he explained with a sigh that he hadn't soiled himself at all.

He went on to say that he was sleeping in the spare room, where all the Xmas presents had been left. He said that during the night he had been rather peckish and had opened a box of *Maltesers*. But, because he was drunk, he had fallen asleep, and for the past few hours had been rolling around the bed on top of the sweets and had inadvertently melted the chocolate all over the bed.

Hallelujah, It was only chocolate. My sentence had just been downgraded from bed linen genocide to petty larceny.

I told him to go and explain to my mum, as I would much rather, she thought he was a thief than a dirty protester.

He did try to explain to her, in the best way he could, and to be honest, she did see the funny side of it, she even titters about it now, oh no – she can't say "titter" can she?

 My dad, however, did not see the funny side of any of it, and still blows steam out of his ears like *'The Flying Scotsman'* every time he recants the tale.

Saturday night fever my arse!

Everyone, no matter who they are, has - at one time or another, made a fool out of themselves. The list of gaffs famous people have made has become part of the very fabric of our society. It's what makes us British.

The general public love to see anybody famous and make a complete arse of themselves.

The more public the humiliation, the louder we cheer. The lower a famous person goes in the humiliation rankings – the more we are endeared to them.

I'm not talking about the Z list of minor celebrities who will do anything to get their beautifully coiffured hair on the cover of OK magazine every week.

I am talking about real celebrities who very occasionally make a mistake.

Take Hugh Grant for example – one minute he is on the BBC world news for blowing like a geyser in the back of a taxi in Hollywood, with a lady of the night, the next he is on Question Time with members of the cabinet and getting louder rounds of applause than the politicians.

Remember that photo of Nick Nolte after he was arrested for being drunk in charge of a motor vehicle? He looked like Johnny Rotten's grandad after he had been mauled by a tiger.

Of course, the best of all gaffs - the Royal gaff, of which Prince Phillip was the tenth dan. His legendary gaffs have left countries on the brink of war. If the Palestinians and the Israelis got on like a house on fire, if Prince Philip visited the region, it would be back to square one. Houses would be set on fire during his visit. He puts his extremely well-heeled foot in it, wherever he goes. But we forgive him, because like some of the pubs I frequent, he is Royal and old.

The most disgraceful behaviour always involves, famous people, being caught with their pants down. George Michael was caught by an off-duty policeman, for performing a lewd act, in the public toilets in that park in LA. What was the off-duty policeman doing there?

It is always the men who are caught with their pants down, never the women. Well strictly that isn't true – I forgot about Paula Radcliffe at the Olympics – What she did took some 'balls'.

Anyway, if famous people make terrible gaffs, what chance do mere mortals have?

The year was 1987 and Miami Vice was still on the box.

I refer to Miami Vice because the powder blue suit and canvas espadrilles I was wearing, whilst slightly flamboyant even for the Wirral, were not classed as a gaff in those days. I thought I looked rather good at the time. Photographic evidence, and a quarter of a century later, I realise it was a fashion catastrophe. *A Faux Pas!*

Powder Blue suits and no socks may look great on Usher in an MTV video shoot, but not walking down the North End for a night out in Birkenhead.

It was my birthday, and I was 24. We were off to The Pleasure Drome nightclub, which at the time had recently opened. It was classed as a fun pub and the DJs wore silly 'Timmy Mallett' baseball caps. It was a place where anything went, dancing on tables, it was very difficult to offend anyone, and almost impossible to get thrown out. That was until I showed up.

I don't know why I tried to get into the nightclub wearing dark sunglasses. It was summer, yes, but it was twilight and overcast.

I wasn't wearing them when I was walking down the road, I just thought it might look cool. Bono might get away with wearing them in an extremely dark nightclub, he may even look cool. But other than that, nobody other than a bloke with a Labrador should be allowed in wearing mirror reflective glasses. I just looked stupid and resembled a Blue bottle.

I had been drinking a lot, but as I was with a crowd, who looked almost sober. They let me in, minus the Bono sunglasses.

It was whilst sitting at the bar in my powder blue suit a colleague told me he had bought me a birthday present. He presented me with a pound of sausage meat. It was a joke and I just said thank you. Took the sausage and put it in my trouser pocket.

I then totally forgot about it. I went back to drinking my *Holsten Pils and cider snake bites.*

Sometime later, I got a call from the DJ who said it was my birthday and that could I make my way to the stage. Even though I was smashed out of my brains I knew getting up on stage, to the baying crowd may be quite embarrassing.

As I climbed onto the stage the DJ started playing the Stripper music, I don't know what the actual name of it is. You know the one – "da da da – tee da dar ......"   The DJ was very enthusiastic and was used to making fools out of people in public. But he was not about to do that to me. Well, that's what I said to myself.

The reality was I didn't need any help from him, as I made a complete arse of myself, as I managed to offend everyone in the nightclub with my amusingly shaped sausage meat.

As the music continued the DJ asked me to start taking my jacket and shirt off. I knew where this was heading, but he didn't.

I needed to get off the stage quickly and by the wolf whistles from him and the crowd, I was going to be making a complete dick of myself for quite some time.

That is when it hit me – Dick – I turned away from the crowd and put the sausage meat down my trousers. I then turned around and to a sound that can only be described as silence. I unzipped my pants and flopped out the 9-inch sausage meat to a stunned crowd. The music was still playing, but the DJ looked on aghast as my 9-inch appendage quickly became 10 then 11 then 15 inches long.

The swaying of my hips and gravity was pulling my enormous, newly acquired phallus closer to my foot.

As tumbleweed rolled across the dance floor, people stood mouths open. I started to quite like the sight of myself 'Donkey rigged'.

A moment later the silence was broken by screams from the crowd, as though an earthquake had shaken the building. I grabbed my enormous manhood and swung it over my shoulder. One girl near the front asked her friend for a chair. She started to buckle.

 Next thing I know I decide to put the end of the sausage meat in my mouth. The other end was still in my zip, so it looked extremely pornographic. I looked like a Grand National winner.

That was the final straw. The DJ who moments earlier had forgotten how to speak English, managed to close his mouth and get his lips to start moving again. My lips were moving too, with a mouth full of uncooked pork and leek.

He shouted, "Ok that's enough – someone please remove him off stage".

Two bouncers came at me from either side and picked me up by the elbow. As I was carried off stage my feet didn't touch the floor, but my enormous cock trailed behind me like I was on a medieval skewer.

As they carried me off the stage across the dance floor to the door that said *Emergency exit*, my manhood knocked over two drinks on a table of four and rested momentarily on the head of a young girl, who started screaming.

I don't remember the bouncers throwing me out, but I do remember waking up on a crowded train to Spital an hour or so later.

I looked down at my pants which were unzipped. The sausage meat had disappeared, as had any dignity I once owned. My powder blue suit was in an unsightly state. I was dribbling uncontrollably and the diabolical sausage meat pate around my midriff had caused people to vacate their seats. A six-foot exclusion zone from my gapping trousers had quickly manifested.

Christ – I've never seen a mess like it. It was like a cow's stomach had exploded and the entrails had landed on me.

John Hurt in that scene from *Alien* when the critter came out of his stomach had a cleaner shirt on than me. Ariel or Daz on a boil wash wouldn't shift the caked-on mess, nor setting fire to myself would get the stubborn stains out of these trousers.

It was then I became aware that every eye on the train was looking at me, but I was too drunk to care.

I tried with some difficulty to zip my pants, but halfway up the sausage meat caused the zip to get stuck. I closed my eyes and drifted off back to sleep.

I never wore the suit again. I had to throw it away. Some say it's the best thing that ever happened to it. However, I still see reruns of the old *Miami Vice,* I see Don Johnson's powder blue suit and espadrilles and hang my head in shame.

You can't wear socks with those shoes!

Steer clear of the brown snow

Nothing can be as exhilarating as the feeling of skiing down a mountain at forty miles an hour, especially when you can't ski. It certainly gets the ticker racing.

Now I am no expert when it comes downhill. But I do know they grade slopes based on an incline.

Green, Blue, Red, and Black, but I never knew they had a brown run until I was skiing in Bulgaria.

I had just mastered a black run and was feeling rather pleased with myself. I thought I cut a dashing figure in my grey salopettes.

As I hurtled down the slope from the top of Mount Musala in the resort of Borovets, I was humming the tune of James Bond in my head. In no time at all, midway between the café at the top and the Hotel Rila at the foot of the slopes, I was not only humming at tune but humming myself, I was farting something awful, which I put down to the stewed prunes and yogurt at breakfast.

I never eat stewed prunes normally, in fact, I hate them, but because it was an all-inclusive buffet-style holiday. I did think, it was a shame to waste them. So, I ate a whole bowl and had cereal and toast and a fry-up.

Unfortunately, I wasn't used to such a formidable line-up of breakfast produce, and in no time at all, it manifested the need to produce something myself, in the lower bowel.

So halfway down a reasonably steep hill, and traveling at some considerable speed, I needed a dump. I suppose I could have held on to it until I reached the bottom, but technically it had already reached 'my bottom'.

I decided the best thing to do, was ski off into a pine forest and expel the breakfast prunes, and anything else left over from yesterday's tea, to make room for the enormous evening meal I was going to eat – Well it was 'All Inclusive'! It would be rude not to. The food would only go to waste.

Waste – was on the top of my agenda as I found a quiet spot to crouch down.

The salopettes were rather snug and I was fearful I might not give myself enough clearance to perform. So, I spread my legs a little further than I should have, whilst still crouching.

What I didn't notice was the ground wasn't completely flat and I started to slide forward, undercrackers around my ankles, my arse not an inch from the skis. I started to panic and imagined myself hurtling down the slope tackle out, coat, ski suit, and manhood flapping.

Ok, flapping may be overdoing the drama, in the cold snow it was more like the nose of a naked mole rat, but you get my drift (snow drift).

I imagined arriving backward across the finishing line to a crowded café of Après Skiers, who were sipping tall mugs of hot chocolate with marshmallows, whilst my marshmallow dragged painfully across the snow, legs akimbo.

So, I was extremely grateful to ski slowly into a fir tree not too far from where I had dropped my trolleys.

I decided the fir tree was a good place to take a dump, it was eco-friendly, private, and more importantly, my fresh 'Tom Tit' would fertilize the roots.

So, in the middle of a Ski resort, three thousand feet up a mountain, in temperatures of minus fifteen, I did my business.

I didn't have any toilet paper but due to paying attention at school, I remembered that snow when melted turned to water. So, I decided the best thing was a wet bum rather than a soiled one. I wiped my bottom with snow.

It wasn't easy to start with, the 'tag nuts' were baked on, but the more snow I applied, the cleaner my ring piece felt. Indeed, the cool snow left a tingle, like a minty tube of toothpaste had been applied to my nether regions. It made my eyes water – I felt alive.

I was just about to attempt to stand up from my crouching position when a dog come bounding out of the bushes. Apply named it a 'Shitsu' and it was headed straight for my bits.

At the time I was rather concerned, as it started to sniff my bum. After all, it was quite a friendly dog and I would have patted it on the head, but for the precarious position, I was in, crouched down, naked from the waist down and balancing on a pair of skis, halfway up a mountain.

It then squatted down next to me, and side by side, the doggie 'did' what doggies 'do' and left a steaming pile of 'doggie do', as we had a crap in unison. Man's best friend indeed!

The proximity of both deposits melted the snow and inadvertently spawned a natural phenomenon, announcing to nature that spring had arrived, causing several large mammals to awake from hibernation.

The dog, meanwhile, finished performing and looked down at its handy work, sniffed it, and then sniffed mine. To add insult to injury the dog cocked its leg and urinated over my skis.

It was only when it had sniffed mine it started to bark.

All I could assume was it was dog speak for "Phew -Christ Almighty and I thought dog food was bad!"

Terrible photographs!

Sadly, on the night I was celebrating my 21st Birthday, the phenomenal acting talent - Diana Dors passed away. It was only after the event, I heard of her demise. To be honest I never realized what a colossus she was, both physically and in vaudeville circles - treading the boards, heavily reinforced boards at that.

The year was 1984, and digital photography was still in its infancy. However, the embryonic seeds had been sown in the form of the 'disk camera'.

Unfortunately, they were all the rage at the time I was given four of them as gifts. Four disk cameras in one night!! I also got three silver tankards.

I decided I couldn't possibly use four cameras, but the film from four would come in very handy, especially when you get two films per camera.

It was then I stumbled upon a brain wave. I would remove the films from three of the boxes and take the cameras back to Dixons.

The problem was the salesperson might open the packet of film and see the top of the silver foil ripped. It was of course in the days before you needed a receipt as proof of purchase.

After pondering my predicament, I decided to fill the foil packet with Jacobs cream crackers. They were the same size and thickness as a disk film.

They slotted in beautifully, and to add to the authenticity, I turned the foil packet upside down in the box, so it looked like the film had been unopened.

I took them back to Dixon's in Northampton and the sales assistant did indeed check the film was in the box before putting them back on the shelf and handing me a credit note for the value.

Of course, he didn't dream that inside, what he assumed was the sealed packet, was a Jacobs cream cracker.

I did laugh when I thought about the three unfortunate people who would buy a disk camera and found to their dismay, that the gift contained two cream crackers instead of a film.

Furthermore – not only would they lose the photographic opportunity, but how could they explain the cracker in the silver foil, when they took it back to complain?

It is so ludicrous the shop assistant might just believe them.

I still laugh now. Imagine receiving a camera for your birthday, excitedly opening the film to take some shots of the big day, only to discover, the only thing you could do with them, would be to butter them and put them on the buffet table.

Sooth my itchy arse

Recently I have moved desks at work, and I have to say, since doing so, I think I have developed a worm.

The problem is, the bloke who sits next to me has a sweet tooth, and if that isn't bad enough, his sister fans the flames, as she works in Greggs the bakers and gets boxes of 'freebies'.

As a result of this bloke's love affair with his sister's sugar-coated delights, there has been an endemic of worm and diabetes-related problems, the likes of which haven't been seen in Rochdale since the Sticky chocolate pudding crisis in the council canteen in 1987. When Cyril Smith ate the entire dessert trolley.

We have tried to tell him to stop bringing cakes in, but the Battenberg cakes just keep coming. His desk resembles an EU food mountain.

Mind you, he is a big lad himself. He looks like Snowdon in winter, only the white stuff on top isn't snow, it is caster sugar. He is so large that we must use specialist climbing gear to stop us from being pulled into his gravity. He has replaced Pluto as the ninth planet in our Solar System.

There are five or six of us at work, sitting side by side rubbing our bottoms on our chairs in unison, back and forth, for hours on end, like seals on a Falkland beach scratching themselves with their flippers.

It manifested itself in the middle of the night when I awoke with the itchiest 'dirt box' I've ever had. I was scratching like a badger with fleas. I just couldn't stop. The more I itched the worse it got.

I scratched so much I broke the skin on my sphincter, and when I looked in the shaving mirror, I had placed on the toilet seat, my 'ring piece' looked like Fidel Castro's beard sucking a lemon.

I decided the only thing for it, was to take a shower. As I stepped into the shower, I noted that my aging fifty-year undercarriage looked decidedly tired in the full-length mirror. I also noted my grey, pubic thatch had started to look like William Shakespeare's thatched cottage after the National Trust stopped paying for the upkeep. It was dishevelled and rather wispy, to say the least.

Sadly, realizing, as I "clocked" my reflection in the mirror - time waits for no man, I forgot all about my bleeding rusty sheriff's badge and lathered my angry crotch in a cooling mint medicated shampoo.

For a moment nothing happened, but by the time the minty foam had worked its way around the back, I sensed it was going to sting. I clenched in expectation. Just how much it stung my anus is something I was not prepared for.

After a series of 'oh's' and 'ah's' - each one louder than the last, I was screaming like an Opera castrato who has just taken a mouthful of air from a helium balloon. Baggage handlers at Ringway, when loading the plane are subject to less noise pollution than the decibels I was forced out of my mouth. The cat which up until then was sleeping peacefully stretched its back legs hissed at me, wagged its tail, and went downstairs.

Placing the shower head between my legs and switching on the cold tap full blast did nothing but move the pain around these most sensitive areas.

My buttocks felt like I had been kicked by a bucking bronco with a nasty attitude. I was swearing like Brian Blessed after accidentally hitting his thumb with a lump hammer.

My eyes were streaming, snorting like a wild stallion, well as I was naked in the shower, perhaps not a stallion. I thought about setting fire to my genitals, it would hurt less, "Lord God have mercy on me – take me from this place". I started to pull the hair I had out of Biffins Bridge. Jesus – I've never known stinging like it. I almost passed out with the pain.

I invented a new swear word 'Haverford West', I submitted the word to the Oxford English press, but they declined the new word on the grounds it might incite feelings of National ridicule in Wales.

I continued squealing like a pig in an abattoir as I stepped out of the shower, walking like a Japanese geisha with her legs bound, clenching a 100 yen note between the cheeks of her arse.

The next time I was in Sainsbury's I bought 'Dove shower gel'. No more tears indeed!!!

The Swiss chocolatier

The Swiss are good at everything. They are the 'big heads' of Europe. People say things like - "Look at the new watch I have bought – it is Swiss you know". "I'm very rich, so rich I have a Swiss bank account". "I got some chocolates for my birthday, Lindt – only the finest, they are Swiss"

What they don't tell you is they make the finest automated public toilets money can buy. These public latrines are so advanced only people with a Ph.D. in Advanced Mathematics can take a 'dump'. Not because they are only situated on the campus of Geneva University and you need a special permit to use them, but just because of the difficulty any person with average intelligence has working out the complexity of them.

North Korea spent less on getting rockets into orbit!

If you are in a hurry for god's sake - don't bother with a public toilet in Switzerland, you won't have time – Get on a local bus or flag down a car and tell the driver to take you to the other side of Switzerland, then walk for five miles, until you reach the foothills of the Alps and crap in a meadow. It's easier, quicker, and far less humiliating.

"The hills are alive with the sound of farting" – Yes, I know it was filmed in Austria, but it works for Switzerland too.

I drank buttermilk by mistake earlier in the day, and whilst I spat most of it out, I did ingest some of it. What is the point of Buttermilk, I have no idea what purpose it serves. You can't drink it, as it tastes diabolical, you can't put it on breakfast cereal as it makes them taste like sweaty feet. Indeed, it spoils everything it encounters (a bit like me). Putting *Dulux white vinyl silk* on cornflakes would taste better.

Anyway, the resultant spasm, in my lower abdomen, spelled danger with a capital D. I did think about going into a posh hotel to use the 'gents', but earlier that week I had been chased off the premises of the Geneva Hilton when the doorman caught me washing my hair in the fountain outside.

It was then I noticed a rather funky metal public toilet. It just needed a Swiss franc to open, and then you were let inside a 'candy shop' of thunder box wonders, the likes I had never seen.

It was summer and the park in which this lavatory resided was heaving with hordes of people. The queue for the 'wonder bog' was very long.

I was frantically waiting to drop a 'Tommy', and by the time I got the 'TARDIS' I was holding on for dear life. I placed the franc in the slot and like Howard Carter entering Tutankhamun's pyramid, I stepped in wide-eyed, and buttocks clenched.

My 'tortoise neck' was playing hide and seek with my underpants. The longer I waited the less it was hiding!

There were more buttons inside than on the Space Shuttle. I felt like an airline pilot sitting in the captain's seat. The problem was this was Switzerland and, the Swiss think they rule the world. As a result, the instructions were only in either -French, German, or Italian. I was rubbish at French in school, and the only German word I know is, rather amusingly – Fahrt.

I don't even bother to acknowledge Italy exists since my divorce.

So..........

Being blessed with an inquisitive mind, I foolishly started to press various buttons. More fool me for dropping my trousers first, who does that when they sit on the toilet – I ask you! I should have learned my lesson and sat on my hands when the first button I pushed flushed the toilet, and I hadn't even 'started' never mind 'finished'.

However, the noise alone was enough to excite the expectant crowd so that they could move forward in the queue. More surprised perhaps that the British were world champions at crapping so quickly, I had locked the door and flushed quicker than Usain Bolt runs a hundred metres.

Sadly, I didn't learn and pressed several others in quick succession.

The door suddenly opened to a curious and expectant crowd. I sat there, with my trousers around my ankles, laying my 'Alexander Bell' and exposed myself to the slightly annoyed, yet perversely amused crowd. The queue was extremely long at this point and several at the front started to laugh and point at me.

I just curled my lip and stared at the floor, desperately hoping everyone would go away and find another toilet.

Not knowing which button closed the door, I embarrassingly fiddled with the buttons, but the door would not close. Just then I hit two buttons and the door swung shut. Thank the Lord!

I gave an audible sigh of relief, but to my utter dismay, the second button I pressed must have opened the door once more. It swung open, but this time I was stretching for the toilet paper. It was utter humiliation. I just smiled a helpless sorry smile. My adoring public in return just whistled and jeered.

Without an ounce of shame, I stood up, and looked out, staring motionless beyond the baying crowd to Lake Geneva and the magnificent Alps beyond. They were like excited Roman plebs at the Colosseum watching two gladiators battle it out.

My confidence at this point was shot. But I remained stoic and as straight-faced as a politician trying to explain an expense oversight to a public inquiry.

One man cruelly gave me a slow hand clap.

A Gladiator with an axe would have been handy. I would have happily let him cut my head off and raise it aloft, to the mob. It didn't seem to matter anymore - nothing else mattered, for inside I was already dead. The final nail in the coffin was when a young excitable twenty-something ran forward, like a teenage Beatle fan with a crush on Ringo Starr and handed me a toilet roll.

I was like a rat in a coal bunker, I was trapped, and I just had to get out of there, how many times can a man be knocked down? From within a voice called to me to swallow my pride – what pride.

So not bothering to take the time to wipe my bottom, I pulled up my pants, and with as much dignity as I could muster, I walked straight out of the toilet, passed the mass of ridicule and laughter, and with a face that resembled a poker player, and with a stiff upper, best of British lip, did what we Brits do best.

 I nodded to the next incumbent, and holding my head aloft sniffed the fresh alpine air and walked swiftly and rather gingerly, if a little squelchy towards the lake.

I knew when I got to the hotel, it wasn't worth saving my 'threadbare shreddies', I didn't even look in them, I stepped straight in the shower, and tried to cleanse my battered soul, and more importantly my battered arsehole, which at that point, as you can imagine was already quite moist.

Thank the lord for wet wipes!

Tarki Belaidakis' piles

When you get to my ripe old age things start to go wrong, things alarmingly drop off, sag, grow where they shouldn't, and not grow where they should.

I used to have long flowing locks of thick brown hair, they called it the Phil Oakey wedge (Human League), and my boyish good looks made me look like Michael J Fox.

Sadly, those flowing locks have now been replaced with well......

nothing, it has all gone, and now in the autumn of my years, approaching sixty instead of getting compliments that I look like a film star (I refer to Michael J Fox). I am now getting insults that I look like a film star but this time Hannibal Lecter.

Still, I suppose that is better than an auntie of mine who was stopped in the middle of Penkridge high street to be told that she looked like someone famous. My auntie blushed in a "thank you very much" kind of way, only to be told that the person she reminded her of, was none other than the transvestite Lilly Savage.

The ironic thing is – she does! (well not know, she sadly died - Paul O Grady I mean, Lilly was killed off years ago)

It must run in the family, as my dad was once stopped in the toilets of the trade union congress. Mid-flow he was asked, "Are you Arthur Scargill" who was at the conference as it happens.

Trying to dry off the wet patch on his beige suit trousers at the communal blower, he politely said he was not, "Then you must be

Paul Daniels?". He does look like the love child of Arthur Scargill and Paul Daniels to be fair – without the "shredded wheat" haircut.

That is the point about middle age, I am bald for the most part and the parts you can see are grey. I suppose I could have resisted the hair loss and had a Bobby Charlton "Comb over", but it would look ridiculous, time waits for no man. What is the point of a bald bloke with a ponytail, it doesn't look good, act your age and shave it off.

A few years back, a girl got off her seat on a bus when I got on. Instead of thanking her, I was rather upset by it, I am still young, I say to myself, but to others, I am a middle-aged man.

Two or three years ago I went to Leeds on a stag do, I found myself in a nightclub, and a girl came over to me and said "Excuse me, there is a man over there bothering me, would it be ok, if I pretended you are my ......" she paused. I thought she was going to say "boyfriend" but instead, she said "Dad!"

When I lived in Sydney, the city not the person. I worked for a computer firm as a computer operator I was in my late twenties and there was a middle-aged bloke I worked with who had the phenomenal name of Tarki Belaidakis, Greek obviously, or Cypriot, but not Northern Cypriot perish the thought.

Tarki told me he suffered from chronic piles and that he would be taking a few weeks off as he was having them cut away. He said that the surgeon who ironically was Greek himself had described them - this is purely medical speak of course, but he described them as the worst case of "arse grapes" he had ever encountered. He said they resembled the chandelier in the foyer of the New York Waldorf Asteria.

These doomsday Haemorrhoids just had to go, there was no time to waste.

As he awoke from the surgery, he was aware that he was face down in the pillow with his buttocks in the air, held upward by some form of a pillow under his midriff.

An "anus horribilis" as her Majesty would no doubt say. (God rest her soul too!)

He was not in pain, due to still being under the effects of the aesthetic. However, he was awake, though not alert, he felt a chill around his "behind". He turned to discover that his arse was bare and exposed like a newborn baby, though not soft and smooth.

Tried to relax as best he could, after all, it isn't every day a surgeon butchers your ring piece.

Suddenly the curtain flew open, dissipating the last shred of dignity he owned, and in traipse a crowd of student nurses with a doctor.

The doctor ushered the class to shuffle closer to Tarki's ring piece and explained that he had been suffering with piles and replaced the term arse grapes with the correct medical term, and was generally looking to "big himself up" – looking for praise on his "handy work" - adding triumphantly "We got the lot".

As he regaled his tale (Tarki not the doctor), I remember thinking "Imagine that" – well thirty years later I now know how he feels.

Recently I had to go to the hospital to have a colonoscopy. They poke a Karcher up your bottom until you can feel it in your mouth. The actual procedure was not as bad as I thought, and though the pipe was alarmingly long, it was uncomfortable rather than sore or painful.

What was sore, however, was my bum hole, twenty-four hours before the procedure. The procedure is what they call an operation when they don't want to scare you.

Scared I was though, as I clutched my buttock fearing to fart.

It started at seven o clock that evening, I had been given two sachets of powder, each sachet had to be drunk twelve hours apart and the instruction booklet that came with the two sachets said in bold print – DO NOT STRAY TOO FAR FROM THE BATHROOM.

Well, that is what it meant.

At first, nothing happened as I drank a litre of this lemon-tasting brew. It lulled me into a false sense of security, for half an hour I was in total control, so much so, I wondered what all the fuss was about and settled down to watch "American Sniper".

I never did finish watching it, for an hour into the film, I too was fighting the "eeebijeebees" talking in fork tongues and wailing like Jihadists.

It was an absolute blitzkrieg, a scrimmage to the "John", as my sorties to empty my bowel increased exponentially.

During those first twelve hours, my toilet paper consumption emptied the linen cupboard of all but one of a six-pack. My ring sting smarted like Tarki's rim after his piles were surgically removed. I was in utter despair, absolute agony, as it continued to pour out of me.

The brown watery stools were replaced with rice water. Gallons of it. They say that a human being is ninety percent water, I can bloody believe it.

I weighed myself the next morning and I had lost in twelve hours an incredulous seven pounds, half a stone. Who needs weight watchers?

There was a momentary lapse of possibly fifteen minutes, whilst I drank the second sachet, the lull before the storm, like the eye of a hurricane passing overhead, or should that be passing down below – total stillness and calm. Then a moment later carnage on the scale of the Krakow ghetto clearance halfway through Schindler's List.

There was no little girl in a red dress, just my sphincter alarmingly red-raw, and tender as a Raymond Blanc blue steak.

As the night wore on, the "squitters" increased like a pregnant woman's contractions, sweating profusely at the thought there was a real chance if sleep came, I would spoil the sheets for sure. If sleep did not come, which was more likely, there was a very real chance I would shit out a kidney. Followed by the rest of my innards.

Finally, I thought by the time it was time to go to the hospital, there would be nothing left of me. A smouldering pair of slippers and a damp patch of sodden skin were once I sat on the toilet.

My appointment was at two in the afternoon, so my dad was picking me up at twelve forty-five. At half-past twelve, I was still emptying my now spent bowel.

As the doorbell chimed and I wiped my bottom for the last time, I limped to the car like Jack Nicholson in the "Shining", without the axe, I didn't have the strength to hold it - clenching my wretched buttocks for all my worth – thankful that the seats in my dad's brand-new car were wiped clean leather.

As it happens, I got from Liverpool to St Helen's hospital without an accident.

The nurse made me fill in a questionnaire and the last question on the questionnaire was – "Do you wear dentures?" Seriously, I asked her "Which way is he going in?"

When the doctor looked up at my bottom with the hose pipe length of cable, he commented whilst looking at the television screen that was now showing the inside of my rectum, "What a nice clean Colon!" – He asked, "Is this the first time you have had the procedure?"

I replied with a whimper "Yes" He smiled and jokingly said, "Mine too".

I almost shat out my kidney

So, if that's what you must look forward to in middle age,

bring on death, please!

FOOTNOTE - I found out they ask if you wear dentures just in case whilst the colonoscopy is taking place they nip the colon and they need to OPERATE immediately.

Shit stinks

The world revolves around laws and rules, let us face it, without rules, there would be no law and order, a lawless nation, a banana republic, with corruption, high prices, and abject poverty, but enough about the post-Brexit UK.

Everyone in a civilized country has house rules, a lot of them, especially in our house. Most of the rules apply to everyone in the house, except my wife, none apply to her at all, some apply to my daughter, some to both of us, but only one applies to me.

It is a simple rule, which I don't particularly agree with, but abide by, as it causes fewer arguments. Anything for an easy life

It is this – DO NOT GO FOR A NUMBER TWO IN THE HOUSE.

That rule could not be any clearer and more straightforward. No room for misinterpretation.

Believe it or not, my wife has told me that my poo smells – well knock me down with a feather, imagine that my poo smells! I had never realized

The rule does not apply to her trappings, which are no more foul smelling than a freshly cooked biscuit, and she has the comfort of pooing wherever and whenever she likes.

 I, however, can't poo whenever or wherever I like, I must hang on for dear life until I find a suitable resting place for my waste product, and it can be anywhere, except my own home.

Well, I say my own home, but it also extends to other people's houses, especially relatives, and one relative with a very weak flush toilet.

I know it is water saving feature of the toilet, but in practice, it is extremely harrowing to know that, if you do need to go in an emergency, it will need to be performed in batches, like a time trial on a bicycle. Probably involved multiple flushes, and an inordinate time spend in the bathroom, to be certain, all the evidence has been removed.

Despite putting a total ban on house poos and a male excrement exclusion zone that stretches from one side of the house to the other, not forgetting we have four toilets in the house, oh no – ALL are out of bounds, she still finds time to complain that I tend to be a bit "windy" in the car. She says things like "Do you need the toilet" or "Why haven't you been to the toilet".

I could say "Ask yourself why - you know why I haven't been, you won't let me, that's why" I then retort "No I haven't been to the toilet, I'd love to - believe me!".

Well of course I am windy in the car, I'm not allowed to expel anything gaseous or solid on the plot of land that constitutes the boundary of our land as dictated by the deeds of the house and held legally by the land registry.

The car is the only place I can be windy!

It doesn't just apply to my home though, oh no, it also extends to anywhere I happen to be with my wife. On holiday, I can't use the bathroom, even though I have paid a lot of money for the privilege of booking a room with an attached bathroom.

On several cruises we have been on, I have been forced to wander the ship, at ridiculously early times in the morning, and often frantically, looking for the public toilet, only found in the public areas near the restaurants, several decks above our cabin, to find they are occupied by another poor sod, who has had instructions from his wife to "dump" the contents of last night's three-course meal over the side. Literally.

I am forced then, to hold on for all its worth, until the joyous, time-critical sound of the latch on the toilet door being unlocked, to enter the domain of someone else's stench, and the indignant act of resting my sad buttocks on an already "warm" seat.

Even worse, whilst you are waiting, cross-legged and sweating, several gents only needing a piss, know you are waiting for a poo, and silently think, why doesn't the idiot "go" in the comfort of his cabin.

All the time this is going on, my wife is "beautifying herself" in the bathroom I should be using and wondering why I have taken so long.

Anyway, back to the story. How it manifested itself was a few years back, I was having a crap in the ensuite, and my wife walked into the bedroom, and in a rather nasty, slightly reviled tone of voice, snarled "Jesus wept – you stink". It was irritating her, and instead of me having a nice, relaxing dump, she then said

"What the hell do you think you are doing?"

I replied a little surprised "I am having a crap".

She retorted "How dare you".

"What? How dare me what" I said, only for an argument to ensue. "How dare you use the toilet".

"What do you mean – that is what it is for isn't it?" "Well, I don't want you doing it in there".

I did raise an eyebrow at this point, and I suppose I was rather sarcastic in my reply "Where do you want me to do it? On the carpet in the bedroom".

And so – here we are a few years later having to do my "business" elsewhere.

Last week I was driving my daughter to an early morning violin lesson when I realized I needed to unload. I knew that there was an ASDA nearby, and I would use their facilities, as I often did on Saturday mornings. I don't shop at ASDA, I shop across the road at ALDI, but ALDI doesn't have toilets for punters. So, I religiously go every Saturday at 8 am, to the number two cubicle in ASDA.   I never buy anything, but I always leave something.

On this morning, I realized I had overbaked my turkey and had miscalculated the timings.

As I got to the ASDA carpark, it was already in the loading bay, and I had started to sweat profusely. I was so close to touching cloth that I barely had time to lock the car door.

It was only at that point I realized how important one-hundredths of a second are – I had only ever thought of them in Grand Prix terms.

I raced into ASDA to find the cleaner was in there, so in a blind panic asked a young shop assistant if I could use the disabled toilet, after all, I was limping badly, but not for the medical reasons she assumed.

A double bonus is, it was early, and being the disabled toilet, not many people use it, especially at 8 am. So more than likely pristine.

Let's face it, anyone needing a disabled toilet whilst shopping would still be taking their medication at home, that early in the morning.

She obliged and as I dropped my underpants with a sense of relief and contentment, with only a few hundredths of a second between an undergarment disaster, I sat in private prayer and thanked Christ I hadn't soiled myself.

I was slightly more relaxed about the fact if I had soiled myself, I was already in ASDA, and GEORGE would bail me out.

As I sat there contemplating life, I realized I was sitting in precisely the same place, as I had been born. I was sitting in ASDA on the grounds of the old Sefton General Hospital on Smith Down Road.

How fitting then I thought, if I die right now on the throne, I would be fulfilling the life cycle of every salmon on the planet, going back to die in the precise spot that they had been born.

Footnote - The thought process I applied about DISABLED toilets being pristine early in the morning, would have shattered the dreams of the person who used the toilet after me, they would have gone in thinking, it is early, and they will have told themselves the toilet rim will be as clean as a whistle, still smelling of the bleach the cleaner squirted into the bowl earlier that morning.

Sadly not, as I shamefully left the pan looking like tigers back. Well, there was no toilet brush, and the toilet paper looked a bit sparse on the roll.

However, talking of Salmon and Tigers, Isn't nature amazing?

Who does love David Attenborough?

FOOTNOTE - If I had the ultimate dinner party I would have to invite the following people.

David Attenborough, Michael Palin, Billy Connolly, and Sandy Torsvik, maybe Frankie Boyle to lower the tone, once Sir David had gone to bed!

I've been driving in my car

Other than purchasing a house, the biggest investment people usually make will be a car.

However, when you are a gormless spotty youth with no common sense and even less money, your judgment can be clouded, and the choice of vehicle is limited.

It sounded feasible I suppose, if not plausible, but knowing the difference between the two, comes with age; when the salesman in the back street garage, who made Arthur Daley look like St Francis of "Asissi", rubbed his chin, sucked in air, and twiddled with his moustache, before declaring he could not go lower than six hundred and fifty pounds for such a fine vehicle.

He coughed and curtailed an enormous laugh, as I signed on the dotted line.

The Vauxhall Chevette that had caught my eye was, from a distance a looker, in the same way, Kingston Jamaica looks charming, from the safety of a satellite orbiting the earth, or a cruise ship anchored a mile out at sea, and night.

He told me it was an Irish import and had been owned by a nun. The fact it was imported meant it possessed a brand-new number plate.

Indeed, it was twelve years old and about as reliable as OJ Simpson in the witness box, which was of little concern to me, as the prospect of driving around in what appeared to be a new car, at the age of eighteen, was all that mattered.

 I wanted it regardless of its flaws, of which there were many.

It's a bit like a bloke who is forty and is still a virgin, who will overlook the fact the woman if indeed it is a woman he is chatting up at the bar, has a six-o clock shadow and is the size of Luxembourg, has webbed feet and is tattooed from head to toe.

If the woman has said yes, then he can gloss over her many faults.

And so, without so much as a test drive, I parted with six hundred and fifty pounds, as the man turned and click his heels and fled for the safety of his portacabin, like a prairie dog running for cover as a golden eagle hovers overhead.

The snagging list started as soon as I pulled off the forecourt.

The steering was a little heavy and pulled to the left sharply when I braked.

When I say brake, it was easier to stop the car by opening the door and putting my feet on the road at thirty miles an hour the brakes did not work. To say they were spongy was a disservice to sea-dwelling invertebrates across the globe.

On my first day, I ran out of petrol, as the petrol gauge did not work and for the year I owned the vehicle, the petrol gauge read half full, so I was forced to guess when I would run out. Unfathomably stressful on the two long motorway journeys I took that year.

Let's face it I had been sold a dud. Only one headlight worked when I switched the lights on, and the other one was in danger of falling out of its housing. I am no mechanic, and couldn't afford one, so held the headlight in place with fishing wire tied to an engine mounting.

This sort of "Do it yourself" initiative is the type of mechanics most of the third world still operate under, due to economic void (anywhere south of Gibraltar).

I remember once being pulled over by the Police for doing fifty miles an hour in a forty zone. The surprise to me was that I was driving at fifty, I didn't think the car was capable.

Anyway, this surly officer told me "I was a danger to society" He said "Do you know how long it takes to stop at fifty miles an hour" I retorted "one hundred and seventy-five feet". He said, "Don't be funny sunshine" I replied sarcastically "well you asked me".

I would say that the stopping distances are on the back of the Highway code so not that difficult to remember, However, that was for a normal vehicle. This Irish import Vauxhall Chevette didn't have brakes and in fact, a Norwegian super tanker would stop quicker.

I kept this unreliable heap of "shit" for a year, before deciding to go around the world. The problem was that after a year I still owed five hundred pounds to the bank.

Over the year, the rust had started to show through it was nine parts rust to one part steel.

The headlight fell out of its housing, and I was forced to hold it in place with fishing wire strapped to the engine mountings.

The oil, well it used as much oil as it did petrol. It was worth absolutely nothing.

I was going to be five hundred pounds out of pocket and the MOT was due.

Solution – find a gormless spotty teenager who would be impressed to own a "virtually" new car whilst still in your teenage years.

My friend who was going around the world with me worked with just such a gullible youngster who as chance would have it, had just passed his test and was looking for a car.

As he signed on the dotted line and parted with four hundred and fifty pounds, I turned and gave it toes. I was only fifty pounds down and free of the money pit.

Two weeks later I left to go around the world.

Several months later my mate who returned to the United Kingdom before me, bumped into the now less gullible teenager in Far Cotton Northampton.

He asked how the car was going. The bloke turned bright red and in a rage through a mouth that spat saliva, as he spoke in a tortured voice, explained that two weeks, just two bloody weeks after I had "disappeared", he had problems with the windscreen wipers and took it to a garage.

The mechanic nearly choked on his cup of tea as the spotty youth asked him to fix it. The man said – and I am only repeating what I have been told "well, to fix the wipers may cost twenty quid, but to put the rest of the death trap right would cost nearly a grand"

The youth blew like Stevenson's Rocket – steam was simultaneously dripping from his ears and nose as he told the less-than-impressed mechanic, that he had only just bought the car.

The mechanic suggested in his professional opinion he should take it back to the person he bought it from.

He said "but I can't" to which he replied in a bemused voice "why not"

"Cos he's left the country" the youth retorted – Now flame red.

The mechanic with no irony in his voice answered: "I'm not bloody surprised!!"

Monkey Business

Believe it or not, your choice I know, but I once had a pet monkey.

Well, I say pet, I looked after one, in return for food and lodging, on the impressively Robinson Crusoe tropical paradise of Tioman in the South China Sea. Burger king has probably opened an outlet there now, and they offer free wifi at every chalet. It is called progress, but I hate it. But not in November 1985.

Now at this point, when I said the monkey, you were probably thinking of a Chimpanzee, that's a little different, they are large, extremely strong, can rip your arm off, and get dangerously aggressive at the drop of a hat. They also throw their shit at each other for amusement and play with themselves all the time. Who doesn't?

No not that kind of monkey. So you are now probably thinking of another type of money monkey – How many can there be – Well, a lot, 260 different species, so carry on guessing - Baboon I hear you say! No, a baboon has a red bottom and extremely large bad teeth, like the man next door but one to me, and causes hundreds of pounds worth of damage to an unsuspecting motorist who is foolish enough to drive their brand new Bentley Azure through the "Monkey Compound" of the Safari Park. Baboons that are, not my neighbour!

No this was a little monkey – with a tail. I think they call them Rhesus Macaques, and in rural Malaysia, it is not uncommon for villages to have a Rhesus Macaque as a communal pet.

So working my way around the world, I arrived in the South China Sea, the day the world discovered that Rock Hudson had died of something no one had heard about – called Aids.

As I had very little money, I used to ask locals if I could earn my keep by working for them in return for food and lodgings.

The head "honcho" was called Nazri and he had a few huts in Tekek Village. It was an amazing place, where you dropped anchor one hundred metres from shore and waded to the beach holding your rucksack above your head. It now has an international airport (probably).

Anyway, Nazri was quite taken with the idea of a "home help", so my offer was taken up instantly. I must admit I was not expecting his response to my request for work, I had half expected him to say "Yes – you can start by unblocking that sweaty Germans toilet, he has been suffering from a bout of Giardia and dysentery for three weeks now, and I just can't shift the stinking feculence from the pipe."

But he didn't – he said, "Come with me, I am going to introduce you to "bimbo" the monkey".

They say romance is dead – well I am not sure who said it, but it certainly wasn't with me and Bimbo.

We hit it off immediately, I may have been the tropical paradise that we both called home, the swaying palms, the gentle lapping of the crystal clear waves onto the talcum powder white sand, the balmy evenings, the constant darkness (when the generator didn't work) or the hundred thousand sparkling stars that lit up the night sky, I just don't know, but we formed a bond that only couples in love could.

We became the best of friends, we laughed, and we sang together, although Bimbo's rendition of Nessum Dorma was a little flat, and several monkey octaves higher than mine.

Bimbo was perfect in every way; I grew to love Bimbo like a mother loves a new born (child not a monkey!!)

I had never been close to a wild animal before, well I know it was technically a "pet" but it wasn't exactly a hamster or a goldfish, dog, rabbit, or hen-pecked husband.

We sat for hours on end de-fleaing each other he didn't have fleas, but they like to groom each other regardless, and the sand on my legs acted as makeshift fleas for Bimbo to pick off and test with his tongue.

Then I would pretend to do the same for him. We had a symbiotic relationship. In human terms, they call it "I'll scratch your back if you scratch mine. We did literally!

After a good long session de-fleaing, he would jump in my lap and take a little snooze. He could sleep for days on end on the lazy log. Snoring for all his worth, well not as loudly as my wife, an emergency coast guard search and rescue drill is not as loud as my wife snoring, but Bimbo slept soundly.

After a week or so of these long naps, Bimbo started to act in a manner that can only be described as "Monkey Business". He was a lone primate, and had needs, and so was I, a primate with needs, but I didn't resort to that kind of "monkey Business", but then again Bimbo was a monkey and he wanted to do his business with me.

So, most afternoons were spent with Bimbo waking from his slumber, sitting on my lap, he would roll on his back and perform an act that most of us wish we could, but very few can, unless dare I say it you are hung like a "Baboon" or some talented gymnast, or perhaps Harry Houdini.

I could do nothing but look on slightly aghast if a little envious. How good would that be to be able at will to roll on your back and... Ok you know where I am heading!

I did try it once myself but didn't get anywhere near, I think I damaged my spine trying, I certainly would need a rib removed to get even close to Bimbo's prowess, in fact in my case I would probably need two ribs removed on either side.

Having two ribs removed did seem rather drastic for a moment of self-gratification. Although thinking about it, I did once date a girl who came from Wallasey and had an extremely flat chest, like a nuns ironing board to be exact, she had saved up five thousand pounds and toyed with the idea of having a "boob job" but at the eleventh hour had a change of heart and had double glazing installed instead.

Anyway, Bimbo could do it as often as he liked and took to it like a duck to water, he pleased himself morning noon, and night.

One day I remember sitting there on the beach, Bimbo on my lap, Bimbo's genitals in his mouth, striding in my direction appeared to be a German tourist, I assumed he was German, as only Germans have the "bottle" to wear "Budgie smugglers" in public.

He stopped at my side to watch this "Simian Spectacle".

For a moment he said nothing, and nor did I, subconsciously trying not to mention how rubbish Eastern European cars were, He was from Berlin, which was behind the Iron Curtain at the time, they built Wartburg's for god's sake, what else would I be thinking of. After a painful silence, he eventually said "Why does he do that?"

I smiled, looked up with a bemused expression on my face, and replied: "I suppose because he can!"

Believe me I have tried it, and sadly I can't get close!

Hats off to Paula Radcliffe

I pride myself on being as regular as clockwork in the trap two departments. I empty my bowels once a day, at five in the morning. So, what are you complaining about, I hear you say!

The trouble is – I don't wake up until six.

Yes, perhaps not truly accurate, but I do seem to go at a particular time every day.

Going to the toilet at an inappropriate time can be most annoying, and if you are Paula Radcliffe, quite embarrassing, as well as causing a stir on news at ten.

I don't object to anyone trying to stay in shape, indeed as we grow older and wider in girth, we should all do a little more rigorous exercise.

Running is an ideal way to keep the weight off. Running might even be useful. I can understand how running a hundred metres may be useful, say if you were catching a bus, and you came around the corner, and there it was at the bus stop. You may well need to run the odd hundred metres quite quickly to catch it.

I can even see how running up to a mile could be a reasonable distance to jog. I mean, you are in a hurry, come around the corner, miss the bus, but have a very important prescription to put into the doctor's surgery, before it closes and it is only a mile away, so you decide to run there.

Under no circumstances would anyone in their right mind be forced to run twenty-six miles. You don't think I might just jog from Liverpool to Manchester, even with a good reason to go there, you would opt for the train or coach. So, in my eyes running a marathon is pointless, unless you were going through a midlife crisis, and needed to prove a point.

A similar thing to Paula Radcliffe's lavatorial *faux pas* happened to a colleague of mine doing precisely what Paula was doing when her need for an evacuation prompted an unscheduled 'shit stop' – rhymes with 'pit stop'.

He was a very fit lad I did the Liverpool Olympic distance triathlon a few years back, but he has gone on to bigger and better things. I had to stop running after an infection from swimming in the River Mersey caused me to lose a testicle. No great shakes, I still have one left.

He is building up to doing the Bolton Ironman, and as a consequence found himself entered in the Liverpool marathon last year.

He was only halfway around the course and was running through the Mersey tunnel when he was struck with the urge to soil himself. There were still twelve miles to go, and he wouldn't be able to coax this squirrel tail back into its dray, not for more than a few miles.

As he came out of the Kingsway tunnel and turned onto Scotland Road, he was starting to have grave concerns. He was already sweating profusely, tired, and sore and this preoccupation of the scatological kind was about as welcoming as a Council tax bill to a squatter.

He forgot all about running, the only thing on his mind was finding a side street to unload his own 'squatter'. He had hoped to set a good time, but right now, he didn't care if the comedy horse and a man in diving boots passed him. He needed to stop and squat himself. He had far more pressing matters to think about.

About halfway up Scotland Road, he was 'touching cloth'. He said the feeling of hanging onto a 'turtles head' for dear life was one of the most upsetting, yet exhilaratingly intense feelings he had ever had. He was frantic, just like a delayed passenger running for a plane that is just about to take off. He was at the point of madness and temporarily lost his mind. It is at times like -not wanting to soil yourself, you could commit murder and no judge in the land would convict you.

As the 'moment of no return' approached he saw a parked van at the side of the road. This was his only opportunity, with no room for error. It was now or never. Like a marksman at the Olympics on his final shot for gold, he needed to time it just right. He ran out of the pack, beyond the crowds waving the runners on to glory.

Crouching behind the stationary vehicle, he felt his glorious moment as he managed to get his shorts down in the nick of time.

It was with great relief that he managed successfully to empty his bowel. He came prepared, as he had stuffed tissue paper in his shorts in case of this precise eventuality.

What he wasn't prepared for was the way he messily voided his bowel – He described it as emptying a tin of semolina onto the pavement.

As he wiped contentedly, slightly conscious that he may not have put enough toilet paper in his shorts - he was aware of a 'presence' around him. He looked up from his squatting position to see the eyes of a six-year-old upon him.

He nodded to the child, as he pulled up his shorts.

As he sped off to re-join the race, the six-year-old called to him. He turned to the boy who was inspecting his 'spending' in great detail.

To his horror, in his madness to get his shorts down in time, he had inadvertently dropped his water bottle in the middle of his feculence.

The child being an ever-the-opportunist Scouser, shouted to him.

"Hey mate –I'll keep an eye on your water bottle for a pound"

The next bit is particularly upsetting, and for those with a nervous nature – look away now!

Instead of saying "It's ok, you can keep it". This colleague of mine, who shall remain nameless – ran back to the steaming welt and picked up a sorry, filthy, 'stool-strewn' water bottle, and carried it for the next hour to the finish line.

The good news is he dropped the water bottle at the finish line and his hapless 'tom tit' rolled over the line seconds before him, and qualified for an official time.

FOOTNOTE – The readers do not know who you are (the culprit), but you have certainly dropped in my estimations.

QUOTATIONS: "I had the ambition not only to go as farther as anyone had been before but as far as it is possible for a man to go" **James Cook RN**. " Do just once what others tell you cannot be done, and you will never pay attention to their limitations again. **James Cook RN** "As life is short and the world is vast – the sooner you start to explore the better" - **Rouen**. "You normally only have seventy years if you are lucky, so the more you cram into your life the better your life will be, do as much travelling as you can, this life is not a rehearsal. **Bartholomew Start**.

I would like firstly to thank everyone who has ever said: "Everyone has one good book in them". I hope you are right. I would also like to thank my dad who in 1984 told me I was a fool to even think about going travelling around the world, and to remember if I got stuck anywhere, don't bother phoning home as he wouldn't bail me out. Thank you, **Dad**, without those words ringing in my ears as I left Dover, I would not have had the adventures and issues I experienced and the adventures that have shaped my life. I would also like to thank **Maria Silker** who said that my stories were very funny and perhaps I should write them down one day. I would like to thank my sister **Bec Foulis** for correcting the plethora of grammatical errors. To **Lynsey** and **Andy** in the DBA team for making my scrawl look like a book. To **Gary Silver Fox Walker** for the subtitle. To **Lisa** and **Susan** for listening to me waffle on about my adventures and laughing in the right places, sometimes out of kindness perhaps. Thank you for laughing with me, not at me. To **Mike Madden** who gave me advice on writing and publishing a book. A big thank you to **Neil Kelly** for his Yoda-like wisdom (not) about travel. To **Siobhan** and **Hannah** for bringing sunshine into my life. I hope Hannah grows up with the same adventurous streak as her tired old dad. Lastly to the children of the 90s who grew up in an age of social media, flying around the globe on a gap year with a credit card and a mobile phone, staying in 5-star hotels, not eating the street food in case they get a "dicky" tummy. They will also have set up a website to record their travels and download Tick Tok and You Tube videos daily. Everyone will know what they are up to every minute of the day as the tell everyone on Face Book or Twitter. Surely that is not travelling. Or am I just old in the tooth. I travelled the first time for 18 months and sent three postcards, not entirely sure one of them arrived. However due to the inefficiencies of Asian countries, I am still hope full thirty-seven years later.

TO BE CONTINPOOED

REVIEWS OF CAUGHT SHORT ABROAD MY U BEND ROMP AROUND THE GLOBE   A very high turd to page ratio. Bartholomew Start makes Tom Shape books look like a reference manual. This is gonzo literature at its best. It will appeal to all blokes love affair with the toilet but may offend the ladies. If this book was improved grammatically, by the pen of a serious copywriter it would not be the hilarious romp it is. Don't change a thing Mr. Smart. If you want Wordsworth buy a poetry book. This is just Bumtastic! **REVIEWS OF CAUGHT SHORT ABROAD MY U BEND ROMP AROUND THE GLOBE** Not so much a book as a collection of buttock-clenching anecdotes. Highlights I loved include Biffins Bridge which is not seen on any map, but may appear in a medical journal. The job interview that never happened. Meeting the in laws in a foreign country and they don't speak English. The Pigs in India. I haven't laughed so much whilst reading a book. A unique take on a travel "log". What a joy. By the way, my wife read a chapter and hated it. **REVIEWS OF CAUGHT SHORT ABROAD MY U BEND ROMP AROUND THE GLOBE** From the pens of what must be Merseyside funniest person nobody knows. This is cringeworthy stuff, very very funny, I have never laughed at any book like I did reading this, virtually a laugh on every page. Sit back, strap in and go with Bartholomew Start on his buttock clenching journey around the globe.

REVIEWS OF CAUGHT SHORT ABROAD MY U BEND ROMP AROUND THE GLOBE If you enjoy toilet humour, this is the book for you. I loved it. It is wickedly funny, and very honost. A little too honest, but we have all been there at one time in our life. Anyone who has travelled to less developed countries will, I am sure empathise with the Author. Christ it happened to me in McDonalds in Manchester. **REVIEWS OF CAUGHT SHORT ABROAD MY U BEND ROMP AROUND THE GLOBE** Read the book in a few hours... still chuckling as I write this. Very very funny. Advisable not to read in public spaces, as onlookers may think you are the mad one. It is rare that a book is produced that has you laughing out loud on virtually every paragraph. Laughter is the best medicine. Can we bottle Bartholomew Start. **REVIEWS OF CAUGHT SHORT ABROAD MY U BEND ROMP AROUND THE Globe** Where have you been all my life, I have a new hero, I want to travel with Mr. Smart. Mankind needs a follow-up. Please, get your rucksack out of the cupboard and go travelling, I can't wait for you to recant your tales of woe.

REVIEWS OF CAUGHT SHORT ABROAD MY U BEND ROMP AROUND THE GLOBE Downloaded this as a freebie on Kindle and I didn't really know what to expect. Needing a change of pace, I gave it a go. Can't recall ever laughing so long and hard, and loud (out loud) I have recommended it to all my friends. At one point I was laughing so much that I had an accident and went to the toilet myself. I wish I could write a chapter on that, but I don't have the mind to be able to think outside the box. What a star you are Smart. **REVIEWS OF CAUGHT SHORT ABROAD MY U BEND ROMP AROUND THE GLOBE** I usually read Thrillers or true-life crime, but I really enjoyed Bart U bend adventures, though my girlfriend thought it was a bit childish. This compilation of short stories is hilarious. I have recommended the book, a strange book at that, to all my friends. It is the perfect holiday read, just short enough to dip into. I loved it 5 stars from me and 1 star from my girlfriend (don't take any notice of her) **REVIEWS OF CAUGHT SHORT ABROAD MY U BEND ROMP AROUND THE GLOBE** Funny, ingenuous, gently erudite, and intrepid – these are the qualities required by the reader intending to plunge into the bidet of the authors mind. The best travel books can alter the course of your life, this one may stop you travelling, but it is safe to say, you will see the funny side and laugh at the most inopportune moment. Forget rough Guides, this is the only travel guide you need!) **REVIEWS OF CAUGHT SHORT ABROAD MY U BEND ROMP AROUND THE GLOBE** I hated it, written by a Frat boy, childish and stupid, and quite offensive. I am a nurse, so used to dealing with these sort of issues, but really, how laborious can the chapters be. Surely no one is that unfortunate 1 star at best.

Printed in Great Britain
by Amazon

23383297R00097